# COHERENCE UNIVERSALISM

COHERENCE UNIVERSALISM

# Biology

*Life as Coherence Under Constraint: Origin, Development, and Evolution Reconsidered*

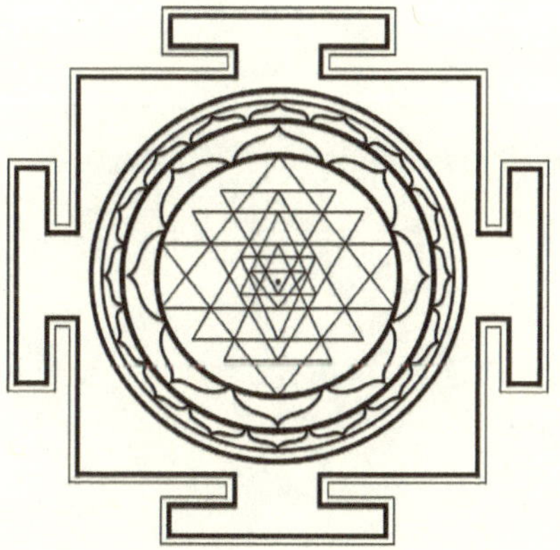

Gaura Kiśora Dās Rader

*Heaven≡Earth Press*

*Coherence Universalism Series • March 2026*

Published by Heaven≡Earth Press
Athens, Ohio

Coherence Universalism Series

ISBN: 978-X-XXXX-XXXX-X (paperback)

This work is part of the Coherence Universalism framework. For the complete series and supporting materials, visit heavenearthfoundation.org.

Printed in the United States of America
First Edition: March 2026

*Dedicated to the vision of a more coherent future*
*for all sentient beings*

# Acknowledgment

*We acknowledge all those who have come before us. Your coherence is not lost, only lost to our vision. Our coherence is made possible only by your coherence.*

Hexagram 13

*Tóng Rén — Fellowship with People*

*Heaven above, Fire below*

*Fellowship with people in the open.*
*Success.*
*It furthers one to cross the great water.*
*Perseverance furthers.*

Fire rises toward heaven: the image of fellowship among people. True community arises not from uniformity but from the clarity that comes when diverse people organize themselves around shared principles. The warmth of fire and the vastness of heaven together suggest that genuine fellowship must be open and inclusive — not confined to faction or clan, but extended to all who share in the common work.

Such fellowship succeeds because it rests on what people hold in common rather than what divides them. It has the strength to undertake great and difficult things — to cross the great water — precisely because its foundation is broad enough to sustain the weight. The perseverance required is not rigid adherence but steady commitment to the shared vision that brought people together in the first place.

*— after the Yi Jing, Wilhelm/Baynes translation*

# Contents

# Section 1: Introduction — Biology as the Study of Coherence Under Constraint


## Abstract

Abstract. This paper applies the Coherence Universalism (CU) framework to biology, proposing that the three great mysteries of the field — abiogenesis, morphogenesis, and evolution — share a common structure: the requirement that integrated organization be preserved across time. The central claim is that coherence, understood as the sustained integration of components, processes, and functions into a unified, self-maintaining whole, is the organizing principle of living systems. The paper introduces a coherence functional $C(x) = A(x) \cdot I(x)$ that decomposes biological coherence into accessibility (aggregate constraint satisfaction) and integration (coupling across subsystems), along with the constraint manifold $K_t$, coherence gradients, and viability conditions. Fourteen substantive sections develop the framework across biological scales: from prebiotic chemistry and the abiogenesis phase transition, through cellular regulation, developmental morphogenesis, and immunological coherence, to evolutionary dynamics reconceived as coherence navigation. The framework yields specific, falsifiable predictions about biological organization, including threshold behaviors in coherence collapse, the relationship between integration failure and cancer, and the dynamical signatures of aging as progressive coherence degradation. Five appendices provide mathematical formalization, modeling results, extended case studies, and a glossary of terms. The paper positions biology as a science of coherence under constraint — the domain in which the physical dynamics of the lower rungs of the Coherence Ladder first become actively self-maintaining.


## 1.1 The State of the Field

Biology confronts three great mysteries. How did life originate from non-living matter? How do organisms develop, maintain, and restore their forms across a lifetime? How does evolution produce adaptive complexity across generations? These questions — abiogenesis, morphogenesis, and evolution — are typically treated as separate problems, addressed by different subdisciplines with distinct theoretical vocabularies. Origin-of-life research asks about prebiotic chemistry. Developmental biology asks about gene regulation and pattern formation. Evolutionary theory asks about variation, selection, and inheritance.

What is missing is not data but integration. Each subdiscipline has produced powerful results, yet the results do not cohere into a unified account of what makes biological organization possible. Systems biology and complexity theory have gestured toward unification, but without an explicit formal criterion for when a system counts as "organized" or "integrated," these gestures remain metaphorical rather than predictive. The field lacks a framework that can say precisely what is preserved when an organism persists, what fails when it dies, and what connects the origin of life to the development and evolution of its forms.

## 1.2 The Preceding Framework

This paper is part of the Coherence Universalism (CU) series, a sequence of papers developing a unified framework in which coherence under constraint serves as the structuring principle across physical, biological, psychological, and normative domains (Rader, 2026b). The Foundations paper establishes the core philosophical and formal architecture — the coherence functional $C(x)$, the coherence gradient $\nabla C$, the **viability constraints**, the principle taxonomy (CU-FP1 through CU-FP9), and the Coherence Ladder that orders domains by logical dependence. The Physics paper demonstrates that coherence dynamics can ground the emergence of time, spacetime, and gravity from a pre-geometric structure, establishing the physical substrate on which biological coherence depends.

The present paper inherits this infrastructure and applies it to the biological domain. The coherence functional developed here is not a new invention but a domain-specific instantiation of the general CU formalism: where the Physics paper treats coherence as structural persistence under dynamical constraint, the Biology paper treats it as integrated self-maintenance (CU-V1) under thermodynamic, metabolic, and regulatory constraint. Readers unfamiliar with the broader CU framework can read this paper independently — the formal machinery is self-contained and the biological arguments stand on their own empirical merits — but the full significance of the results emerges within the series context.

## 1.3 Position on the Coherence Ladder

The Coherence Ladder arranges domains by logical dependence: each rung presupposes the structural conditions established by the rungs below it. Biology occupies a distinctive middle position — above physical coherence (passive persistence under energetic favorability) and below psychological coherence (representational self-modeling and predictive integration).

The critical threshold is the transition from physical to biological coherence: the moment at which passive persistence becomes active self-maintenance. This transition — the abiogenesis threshold — marks the first point on the ladder where a system's continued coherence becomes a governing constraint on its own dynamics. Below this threshold, structure persists only so long as boundary conditions allow. Above it, structure causes its own persistence.

Within the biological regime, the ladder identifies several sub-rungs: far-from-equilibrium structure, metabolic coherence, self-maintenance, adaptive constraint satisfaction, and life itself (see Appendix C for the full development). The present paper addresses all of these, with particular attention to the abiogenesis threshold (Section 4), the **coherence drive** that sustains biological organization (Sections 5–9), and the evolutionary dynamics that refine it (Section 10).

Biology's position on the ladder has a specific consequence for the framework as a whole: it is the first domain in which coherence can be empirically operationalized and experimentally tested. The predictions in Sections 2, 4, and 13 are not philosophical conjectures but experimental programs. If the biological instantiation fails, the framework loses its primary empirical grounding.

## 1.4 The Central Claim

This paper argues that the three great mysteries of biology — abiogenesis, morphogenesis, and evolution — share a common structure.

What unifies them is not a shared mechanism but a shared constraint: the requirement that integrated organization be preserved across time. Living systems persist without stasis. They change continuously — replacing molecules, remodeling tissues, adapting to perturbation — yet remain themselves. From the molecular scale of metabolism to the organismal scale of development and behavior, biological systems operate far from thermodynamic equilibrium. They must actively counteract entropy, repair damage, regulate internal states, and coordinate processes across multiple spatial and temporal scales. Failure to do so results not in gradual degradation but often in abrupt loss of function, loss of identity, or death.

The central problem of biology, on this view, is not merely how life originates or reproduces, but how coherence is preserved under constraint. Here coherence refers to the sustained integration of components, processes, and functions into a unified, self-maintaining whole. Coherence is not static order, nor is it mere stability. It is dynamic, adaptive, and continually renegotiated in response to perturbation. Living systems must remain sufficiently integrated to persist, while remaining sufficiently flexible to adapt.

The three great mysteries become three faces of a single principle: abiogenesis is the first emergence of self-maintaining coherence; morphogenesis is the real-time enforcement of coherent form within individual organisms; evolution is the long-term refinement of coherence-preserving architectures across generations.

## 1.5 The Biology Crisis as a Coherence Crisis

Contemporary biology faces a paradox: it has never been more empirically productive, and yet it has never been less theoretically unified. Genomics, proteomics, systems biology, evo-devo, and astrobiology each generate extraordinary data, but the results accumulate without converging on a shared explanatory framework. The fragmentation is not merely sociological — it reflects a genuine theoretical gap.

The gap is this: biology lacks an explicit criterion for biological organization. We can sequence a genome, model a metabolic network, trace a developmental trajectory, and reconstruct a phylogeny — but we cannot say, in general terms, what it is that all of these processes preserve. "Fitness" is too narrow (it reduces organization to reproductive success). "Complexity" is too vague (crystals are complex; corpses are complex). "Information" is too abstract (it does not distinguish life-sustaining information from noise).

This paper proposes that the missing criterion is coherence — specifically, the integrated satisfaction of viability constraints across multiple scales and timescales. The fragmentation of biology is, on this reading, a coherence crisis in the field itself: an inability to see that homeostasis, development, immunity, regeneration, adaptation, and evolution are all expressions of the same underlying requirement. The coherence functional C(x) developed in Section 2 is offered as a first formal attempt to fill this gap.

## 1.6 What This Paper Does and Does Not Claim

The CU framework does not replace established biological theory. Evolution by natural selection, molecular genetics, systems biology, and thermodynamics remain indispensable. What is proposed is a reinterpretation of their relationship. Rather than treating biological order as the outcome of isolated mechanisms, we treat it as the result of persistent constraints on what can remain viable. Selection does not create coherence from nothing; it filters and stabilizes systems that are already capable of maintaining it.

The mathematical framework developed in Section 2 is offered as a proposal — a formal structure that the author believes captures the right conceptual architecture, and that has been checked for internal consistency and biological plausibility, but that has not been fully vetted by professional mathematicians. The formalism is presented in the spirit of CU's own epistemology: as an invitation to engage, improve, and critique, not as a claim to finality.

Biology occupies a distinctive middle ground between physics and cognition. Like physical systems, living organisms are governed by lawful dynamics and energetic constraints. Like cognitive systems, they exhibit adaptive, context-sensitive behavior oriented toward persistence and repair. Yet biological systems need not invoke meaning, representation, or consciousness to explain their fundamental organization. Their intelligence, insofar as it exists, is embedded in their capacity to maintain coherence under real-world conditions. This paper remains within the biological domain and does not make claims about consciousness, ethics, or social organization — those extensions are developed in their respective papers within the CU series.

## 1.7 Plan of the Paper

This paper develops its argument systematically across fourteen sections. Section 2 formalizes coherence as a dynamical property of living systems, introducing the coherence functional C(x), the integration measure I(x), viability constraints, coherence attractors, and collapse dynamics within a mathematically explicit framework. Section 3 examines the thermodynamic conditions under which coherence maintenance becomes possible. Section 4 analyzes the origin of life as a **coherence phase transition** — the moment at which matter first begins preserving its own constraint structure across time. Sections 5 through 9 examine how coherence drives regulation and repair within individual lifetimes: the coherence drive in living systems (Section 5), multi-scale organization (Section 6), development and morphogenesis (Section 7), embedded intelligence (Section 8), and novel problem solving (Section 9). Section 10 addresses evolution as coherence flow across generations. Section 11 develops a minimal biological epistemology. Section 12 contrasts biological and artificial systems. Section 13 presents testable predictions and an experimental program. Section 14 discusses limitations and conclusions.

The five CU Biology Principles — CU-B1 (Integrated Constraint Satisfaction), CU-B2 (Active Coherence Maintenance), CU-B3 (Adaptive Reorganization), CU-B4 (Evolutionary Coherence), and CU-B5 (Functional Definition of Life) — are developed across these sections and formalized in Appendix B.

## 1.8 What Would Prove This Framework Wrong

The coherence framework is falsifiable. Four classes of evidence would constitute serious disconfirmation:

First, if biological systems routinely exhibit high aggregate constraint satisfaction without integration — that is, if they can maintain all their individual subsystems independently while lacking any coupling between them — then the coherence functional's emphasis on integration (the I(x) term) would be empirically unjustified. The prediction is that integrated organization, not mere aggregate function, is what distinguishes living from nonliving systems.

Second, if the abiogenesis transition cannot be characterized as a phase transition in coherence dynamics — if there is no sharp dynamical threshold between passive persistence and active self-maintenance — then the framework's account of life's origin (Section 4) would fail. The prediction is testable through synthetic biology: systems that cross the recurrence threshold should exhibit qualitatively different dynamical behavior from those that do not.

Third, if organisms solve novel problems (Section 9) by mechanisms that are entirely uncorrelated with their **coherence landscape** — if adaptive reorganization under novel stress has no relationship to the system's constraint structure — then the framework's central explanatory claim would be undermined.

Fourth, if evolutionary dynamics select for traits that systematically reduce organismal coherence without compensating gains at other scales, the framework's account of evolution as coherence flow (Section 10) would require fundamental revision.

These conditions are developed further in Section 13, which specifies the experimental protocols that could test them.

# Section 2: Mathematical Framework — Coherence as Integrated Constraint Satisfaction

To treat coherence as a genuine biological constraint rather than a loose metaphor, it must be expressible within a formal dynamical framework. This section develops a mathematical structure for describing how biological systems maintain, lose, and recover coherence over time. The goal is not merely to gesture at formalism, but to provide machinery that could, in principle, be applied to real biological systems and yield testable predictions. The central insight is that biological coherence is not reducible to any single measure of order, stability, or function. Rather, coherence emerges from the integration of multiple constraint satisfactions into a mutually reinforcing structure. A system can satisfy many requirements individually while remaining globally fragile; what distinguishes living systems is that their constraint satisfactions support one another.

## 2.1 General Approach and Conceptual Foundation

We represent a biological system at time t by a state vector $x(t) = (x_1, x_2,$ \ldots , $x_n)$, where each component corresponds to a biologically relevant variable. The system evolves according to dynamics $dx/dt = F(x, e, t)$, where F captures intrinsic dynamics and e represents environmental inputs. What distinguishes the present approach is the introduction of an explicit coherence functional $C(x)$ defined over state space. High $C(x)$ corresponds to states supporting coordinated function, persistence, and repair; low $C(x)$ corresponds to fragmented or nonviable states; $C(x) = 0$ corresponds to loss of biological identity. The coherence functional induces a gradient $\nabla C(x)$ over state space, defining directions in which coherence increases or decreases. Adaptive behavior corresponds to system dynamics that tend to move the system toward higher coherence—not through representation or foresight, but through the interaction between dynamics and viability constraints. This general framework provides the conceptual foundation.

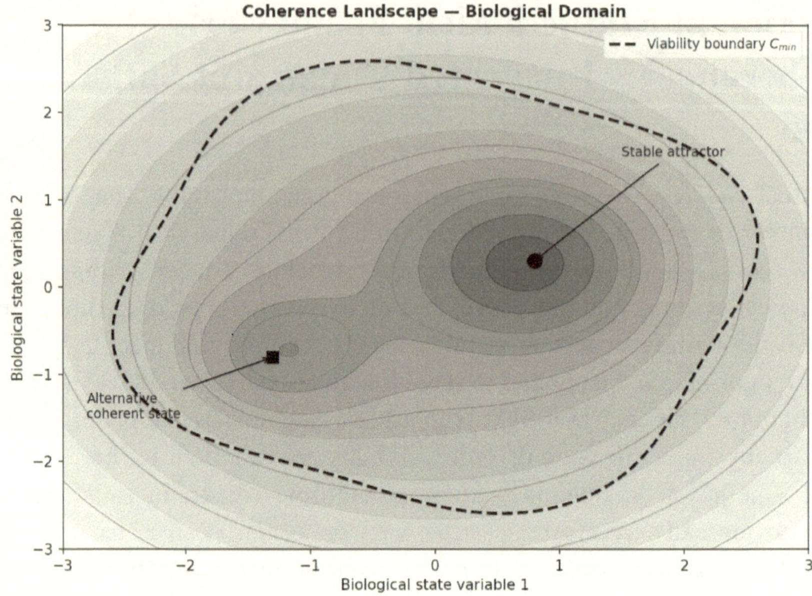


*Figure 1. The coherence landscape C(x) over a two-dimensional state*

space. Peaks (blue) correspond to coherence attractors — stable biological forms. The collapse basin (dark red) represents states below the viability boundary C_min. White arrows indicate the coherence gradient that guides biological dynamics. The spiral trajectory shows recovery from perturbation: the system follows the gradient back toward the attractor without explicit computation.

The following sections develop a more precise operationalization that could, in principle, be applied to specific biological systems and generate quantitative predictions.

## 2.2 State Space and Viability Constraints

The system is subject to a set of viability constraints {$V_1$, $V_2$, \ldots , $V_m$}, where each constraint specifies conditions for continued biological function. Examples include metabolic constraints (ATP production must exceed consumption), structural constraints (membrane integrity), regulatory constraints (gene expression within viable ranges), and thermal constraints (temperature within functional bounds).

For each constraint $V_i$, we define a satisfaction function $v_i: X \rightarrow [0, 1]$, where $v_i(x) = 1$ indicates full satisfaction, $v_i(x) = 0$ indicates critical violation, and intermediate values indicate proximity to constraint boundaries.

## 2.3 The Naive Aggregation Problem

A first attempt at measuring coherence might simply aggregate constraint satisfactions:

$C\_naive(x) = (1/m) \Sigma_i v_i(x)$ But this naive measure misses something essential. Consider two systems with identical C_naive. In system A, constraint satisfactions are independent—perturbing one has no effect on others. In system B, satisfactions are coupled—they rise and fall together. System B is more coherent in the biological sense: it has integration. This observation motivates the central formal move: coherence is not aggregate satisfaction but integrated satisfaction.

## 2.4 The Coherence Functional

Define the coherence functional as:

$C(x) = A(x) \cdot I(x)$

where A(x) is an adequacy term measuring aggregate constraint satisfaction, and I(x) is an integration term measuring mutual support among satisfactions. The adequacy term is defined as the geometric mean:

$A(x) = (\Pi_i v_i(x))^\wedge(1/m)$

The geometric mean enforces a crucial property: if any single constraint falls to zero, adequacy falls to zero regardless of other satisfactions. This captures the biological reality that certain violations are catastrophic.

## 2.5 Formalizing Integration

Integration can be characterized through three complementary approaches that converge on similar formal structures.

### *2.5.1 The Coupling Approach*

Consider the Jacobian matrix of constraint satisfactions: J_ij = ∂vᵢ/∂xⱼ. The constraint coupling matrix Γ_ik = Σⱼ J_ij · J_kj measures how constraints respond to the same state variables. Define coupling strength $\gamma(x) = (1/m^2)\ \Sigma_{i,k}$ \|Γ_ik\|.

### *2.5.2 The Synergy Approach*

Treat constraint satisfactions as random variables under perturbations. Synergy S(x) measures how much the joint distribution carries beyond individual distributions—whether constraints "know about" each other in ways not reducible to individual relationships with the environment.

### *2.5.3 The Robustness Approach*

Define robustness R(x) based on whether perturbations cascade or are absorbed. The fragility matrix F_ik measures correlated constraint violations under perturbation; $R(x) = 1 - (1/m^2)\ \Sigma_{i\neq k}$ \| F_ik(x)\|.

### *2.5.4 The Composite Integration Measure*

The composite measure combines all three:

I(x) = (γ(x) · S(x) · R(x))^(1/3) Integration requires coupling (shared dependencies), synergy (mutual information), and robustness (cascade resistance).

## 2.6 Multi-Scale Coherence

Biological systems are hierarchically organized. Let the system be decomposed into scales s ∈ {1, \ldots , S}. At each scale, define scale-specific coherence C^(s). Cross-scale integration I_cross measures whether coherence at one scale supports coherence at adjacent scales. Global coherence is:

C_global(x) = ($\Pi_s$ C^(s)(x^(s)))^(1/S) · I_cross

This enforces the Local-Global Coherence Principle: global coherence requires coherence at each scale and integration across scales. High coherence at one scale that destroys coherence at another results in low C_global.

## 2.7 Coherence Dynamics

### *2.7.1 The Coherence Gradient*

The gradient $\nabla C(x)$ defines a coherence landscape. Biological systems do not explicitly compute this gradient; their dynamics tend to move along it because configurations that move against it fail to persist.

### *2.7.2 The Update Rule*

Biological systems exhibit coherence-guided update:

$$dC/dt \geq -\lambda C + \eta(e)$$

where $\lambda$ represents entropic degradation and $\eta(e)$ is environmental forcing. This is the biological specialization of the Universal Flow Equation (CU-D1); the Physics paper develops the general form

$$dC/dt = \alpha(\nabla C \cdot v) - \beta(dS/dt) + \gamma\Lambda$$

of which the biological viability condition captures the constraint that living systems must maintain coherence above a minimum threshold. Coherence is actively maintained against degradation.

## 2.8 Attractors, Biological Identity, and the Persistence of Form

Stable biological forms correspond to coherence attractors — regions of state space where $C(x)$ exceeds a viability minimum, trajectories remain stable under perturbation, and the coherence gradient $\nabla C$ points inward. When a system occupies such a region, small perturbations are corrected by the system's own dynamics: the coherence gradient drives the system back toward the attractor's center rather than away from it. Each attractor has a basin of repair measuring resilience — the maximum perturbation magnitude from which the system can recover. Biological attractors are deformable, history-dependent, and nested across scales.

### *2.8.1 Identity as Constraint-Preserved Continuity*

Biological identity corresponds to attractor membership, but this statement requires careful elaboration. An organism is not a static configuration of matter. It is a dynamical process — a trajectory through state space that remains within a coherence-preserving region despite continuous material turnover. Atoms are replaced, cells divide and die, tissues remodel, and yet the organism persists. What persists is not material composition but constraint structure.

Define the constraint manifold $K_t$ as the set of viable future states accessible to the system at time t:

$K_t = \{x \in X : C(x) > C_{min}$ and x is dynamically reachable from $x(t)\}$

The organism's identity is the continuity of K across time (CU-V2, identity-binding integration). Identity persists when:

$D(K_{t+1}, K_t) \approx 0$

even when the physical state x(t) changes substantially. The constraint manifold deforms slowly and continuously — through growth, development, aging — while the material substrate turns over rapidly beneath it.

This formulation resolves a longstanding puzzle. A human body replaces approximately 98% of its atoms within a year. Many tissues regenerate entirely. Yet identity persists. The resolution is that identity does not reside in atoms, cells, or even particular molecular configurations. It resides in the constraint structure that governs which configurations are viable and how the system transitions among them.

Three examples illustrate the independence of identity from material substrate.

First, metabolic continuity. The specific molecules performing glycolysis at this moment will be degraded and replaced within hours. Yet the metabolic network — the constraint structure governing which reactions occur and in what proportions — persists across decades. The organism maintains the same metabolic identity through continuous molecular replacement.

Second, regeneration. Levin's planarian experiments (§2.13) demonstrate the point dramatically. A planarian cut in half regenerates a complete organism. Every cell in the regenerated head is new. The molecular composition is different. The gene expression pattern was transiently disrupted. Yet the organism maintains $K_{planarian}$ — the same constraint manifold, the same attractor — throughout. Regeneration is identity preservation under extreme perturbation.

Third, metamorphosis. An insect undergoing complete metamorphosis dissolves most of its larval body plan and reconstructs an entirely different morphology. The caterpillar and the butterfly share almost no cellular continuity. Yet $K_{organism}$ persists — the constraint structure governing viability transitions smoothly from one body plan to another, even as the physical instantiation changes radically.

### *2.8.2 Why a Copy Is Not the Same Organism*

This framework clarifies a question that purely informational accounts of identity cannot resolve. Suppose every molecule in an organism were duplicated exactly, producing a structurally identical copy. The copy shares the same physical state $x(t_0)$ and the same instantaneous constraint structure. Yet it is not the same organism.

The issue is not merely practical (that the copy will encounter different perturbations and therefore diverge empirically). It is constitutive. Identity is not a property of a state but of a trajectory through state space. Two rivers may share identical water chemistry at a given instant without being the same river; what constitutes a particular river is the continuous flow through a particular channel, not any snapshot of its composition. Similarly, what constitutes a particular organism is the continuous maintenance of K through a particular causal history — the specific sequence of perturbations absorbed, repairs executed, and developmental constraints navigated.

The original organism's constraint manifold K was shaped by its particular developmental trajectory, its history of perturbations and repairs, its accumulated adaptive modifications. The copy begins a new trajectory. Even if identical at $t_0$:

$K\_copy(t_1) \neq K\_original(t_1)$

This divergence is not accidental but necessary, because K is not a static structure that can be copied but a dynamical process that must be continuously sustained. Identity, on this account, is token identity — the identity of this particular standing process — not type identity — the identity of any system with this structure. Copying the structure produces a new token of the same type, not a continuation of the original.

### *2.8.3 The Organism as Standing Process*

The constraint-continuity view of identity suggests a different metaphor for living systems. An organism is closer to a whirlpool, a flame, or a standing wave than to a machine or an object. Remove water and the whirlpool vanishes. Remove fuel and the flame goes out. But no molecule was the whirlpool or the flame. What persisted was a pattern of organization — a dynamical process that maintained itself through continuous material throughput.

Similarly, no molecule is the organism. The organism is the process by which a particular constraint structure is maintained across changing material substrate. This is not a poetic analogy but a precise dynamical claim: the organism is a persistent solution to its own boundary conditions.

### *2.8.4 Death Defined Precisely*

Death, within this framework, is not molecular destruction. It is the irreversible loss of the constraint manifold:

$K_t$ is no longer reconstructible from available dynamics

The system can no longer return to its viable region. All biological definitions of death — cardiac death, brain death, cellular death — become special cases of this general condition: the particular constraint structures governing cardiovascular coherence, neural integration, or cellular metabolism have been irreversibly disrupted.

This definition clarifies borderline cases. A frozen embryo is not dead because K remains reconstructible upon thawing. A patient under deep anesthesia is not dead because K persists despite the temporary cessation of conscious activity. An organism in cryptobiosis (tardigrades, brine shrimp cysts) is not dead because K is preserved in a quiescent form that can be reactivated. In each case, identity persists because the constraint structure governing viable trajectories remains intact, even though active coherence maintenance is temporarily suspended.

## 2.9 Coherence Collapse

### *2.9.1 The Collapse Threshold*

Define a critical integration threshold $I_{crit}$ below which coherence cannot be maintained. Below threshold: constraint violations propagate, recovery mechanisms fail to coordinate, and positive feedback drives disintegration.

### *2.9.2 Cascade Dynamics*

Below threshold, the system exhibits cascade dynamics:

$$dI/dt = -\kappa \cdot (I_{crit} - I) \cdot I$$

for $I < I_{crit}$

Integration continues to degrade; collapse proceeds rapidly once threshold is crossed.

### 2.9.3 Types of Collapse

— Fragmentation: Integration fails while adequacy remains temporarily high (precursor state) — Exhaustion: Adequacy degrades while integration is maintained (resource depletion) — Catastrophic: Both fail simultaneously (acute trauma) — Transformation: System exits one attractor and enters another (differentiation, disease)

## 2.10 Memory and Path Dependence

The coherence functional may depend on history H: C(x, H). This introduces irreversibility— systems in the same state may differ in coherence depending on trajectory. Memory enters through structural modifications, regulatory priming, and experience-dependent coupling changes.

## 2.11 Thermodynamic Grounding

### 2.11.1 The Maintenance Cost

Maintaining coherence requires free energy: $\Phi(x) = \Phi\_A(x) + \Phi\_I(x)$, where $\Phi\_A$ maintains adequacy and $\Phi\_I$ maintains integration. Keeping constraints coupled requires continuous energy investment.

### 2.11.2 Coherence Efficiency

Define coherence efficiency $\eta\_C = C(x)/\Phi(x)$. Biological systems are shaped by selection to achieve high efficiency—maintaining coherence with minimal energetic cost. This efficiency is thermodynamically bounded.

## 2.12 A Toy Model: Three-Constraint Cellular Coherence

To demonstrate the framework concretely, we develop a minimal model with three state variables: $x_1$ (ATP concentration), $x_2$ (membrane potential), and $x_3$ (protein folding quality), each normalized to [0, 1].

### 2.12.1 Model Setup

Three viability constraints: $V_1$ (metabolic), $V_2$ (electrical), $V_3$ (proteostatic). Satisfaction functions: $v_1(x) = x_1$, $v_2(x) = 4x_2(1-x_2)$, $v_3(x) = x_3$.

### *2.12.2 Constraint Coupling*

Constraints are coupled: ATP affects membrane maintenance and proteostasis; membrane potential affects ATP production; protein quality affects all functions. Dynamics include homeostatic restoration and inter--constraint coupling.

### *2.12.3 Computing Coherence*

Adequacy: $A(x) = (v_1 \cdot v_2 \cdot v_3)$^(1/3). Integration: $I(x) = 1 - 1.5 \cdot \text{range}(\{v_i\})$, measuring how "together" the constraints are.

### *2.12.4 Model Behavior*

The model exhibits: (1) stable coherent states, (2) recovery from small perturbations, (3) collapse from large perturbations that break integration, and (4) a fragility phase where I declines while A remains stable.

## 2.13 Connection to Levin's Experimental Program

The framework makes direct contact with Michael Levin's experimental work on bioelectricity, regeneration, and morphological computation (Levin, 2014; Levin, 2021).

### *2.13.1 Bioelectric Patterns as Integration Carriers*

Bioelectric patterns are interpreted as integration carriers—encoding not just target states but the coupling structure between constraints at different locations. Disrupting patterns should decrease I even when local satisfaction is preserved.

### *2.13.2 Planarian Regeneration as Attractor Re-entry*

Planarian regeneration is interpreted as attractor re-entry: fragments retain sufficient integration information to navigate back to the body plan attractor, following coherence gradients rather than reading blueprints.

### *2.13.3 The Xenobot Experiments*

Xenobots demonstrate that cells can self-organize into novel configurations by navigating coherence landscapes—supporting the claim that form emerges from coherence navigation, not genetic programming (Kriegman et al., 2020).

### *2.13.4 Cancer as Coherence Disintegration*

Cancer represents loss of cross-scale integration: cells maintain local coherence while losing integration with tissue and organismal scales. Re-establishing bioelectric integration can normalize cancer cells without killing them (Levin, 2021).

### *2.13.5 Specific Experimental Predictions*

— Integration metrics should decline before morphological abnormalities appear — Regeneration quality should correlate with integration preservation, not just adequacy — Cancer normalization should restore integration metrics before morphological normalization — Xenobot self-organization should follow coherence gradients

## 2.14 Computational Simulation of Coherence Dynamics

Numerical simulations validate that the framework produces predicted dynamics. The threeconstraint model was implemented with parameters calibrated to show biologically plausible behavior.

### *2.14.1 Result 1: Stable Coherent State*

From initial conditions, the system converges to a stable state with $C^* \approx 0.45$, approaching equilibrium along coherence gradients (Figure 2).

### *2.14.2 Result 2: Perturbation and Recovery*

Small perturbations: system returns to stable state. Large perturbations that push I below threshold: cascade collapse ensues (Figure 3). The threshold behavior is sharp—a key signature of the framework.

### *2.14.3 Result 3: The Fragility Phase*

Under chronic stress, integration declines while adequacy remains temporarily stable—the “fragility phase.” Standard health metrics appear normal, but resilience is lost. A perturbation easily absorbed earlier now triggers collapse (Figure 4).

#### *2.14.4 Result 4: Cascade Dynamics*

Below threshold, I decays approximately exponentially, consistent with the cascade equation. The measured decay rate $\kappa\_eff \approx 0.024$ demonstrates the predicted dynamics (Figure 5).

#### *2.14.5 Result 5: Multi-Scale Extension*

A two-scale model shows that local optimization (cell level) that ignores global constraints (tissue level) produces temporary C_cell increases but eventual C_tissue collapse, followed by global failure. This models cancer dynamics (Figure 6).

#### *2.14.6 Connecting Simulation to Biological Observation*

Simulation results map to biological phenomena: stable state → homeostasis; small perturbation recovery → normal stress response; large perturbation collapse → acute trauma; fragility phase → subclinical decline; multi-scale divergence → cancer.

## 2.15 Testable Predictions

The framework generates specific, falsifiable predictions: 1. Integration precedes collapse: Before failure, I should decline while A remains stable. This predicts measurable “fragility phases.” 2. Recovery follows integration gradients: Systems should restore integration before optimizing individual constraints. 3. Cross-scale coherence bounds adaptation: Local adaptations that damage global integration should be unstable. 4. Coherence efficiency predicts evolutionary success: Lineages with higher $\eta\_C$ should show greater persistence. 5. Bioelectric signals carry integration information: Disrupted bioelectric patterns with preserved morphology should show fragility.

## 2.16 Relation to Existing Formalisms

The framework connects to established approaches while remaining distinct: — Integrated Information Theory (IIT): Related but distinct—I measures integration of constraint satisfactions, not information integration per se (Tononi, 2004). — Free Energy Principle (FEP): Compatible but different emphasis—FEP focuses on prediction error; coherence focuses on constraint integration (Friston, 2010). Viability Theory: Extended by adding integration structure to constraint satisfaction. — Autopoiesis: Coherence operationalizes autopoietic organization quantitatively (Maturana & Varela, 1980).

## 2.17 Limitations and Open Questions

Important limitations remain: measurement challenges (computing coherence in real systems), parameter specification (determining system-specific values), computational complexity (especially for synergy measures), scale selection (decomposition choices), and validation (systematic empirical testing needed). These represent opportunities for future development.

## 2.18 Summary

This section developed coherence as integrated constraint satisfaction: viability constraints with satisfaction functions; coherence = adequacy × integration; integration via coupling, synergy, and robustness; multi-scale coherence requiring cross-scale integration; coherence dynamics with gradient-following update; attractors encoding biological identity; collapse via threshold-crossing cascade; thermodynamic grounding with efficiency bounds; a toy model demonstrating the

mathematics; connection to Levin's experimental program; simulation validation; and testable predictions. The framework transforms coherence from suggestive metaphor into quantitative research program—machinery for asking precise questions about biological organization that can be answered through measurement and experiment.

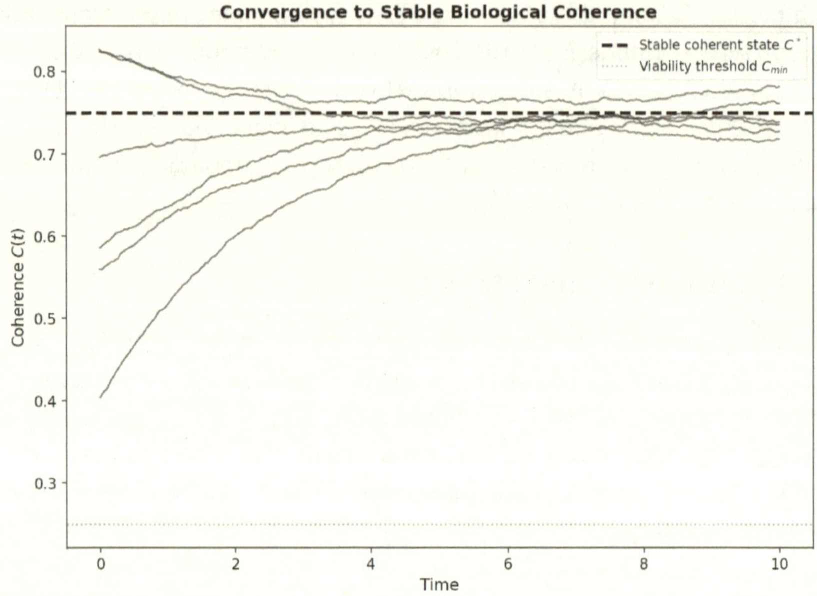


***Figure 2.*** *Convergence to stable coherent state. Top: State variables*

x1 (ATP), x2 (membrane potential), x3 (protein quality) converging to equilibrium. Bottom: Coherence metrics A (Adequacy), I (Integration), C (Coherence) stabilizing at their equilibrium values.

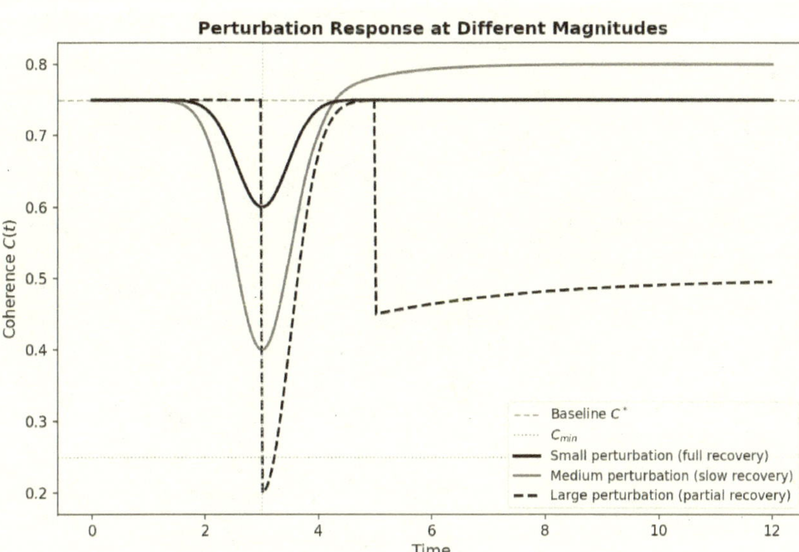


***Figure 3.*** *Perturbation response at different magnitudes. Small and*

medium perturbations recover to the stable coherent state. Large perturbation pushes Integration below the critical threshold I_crit, triggering cascade collapse to the non-viable attractor.

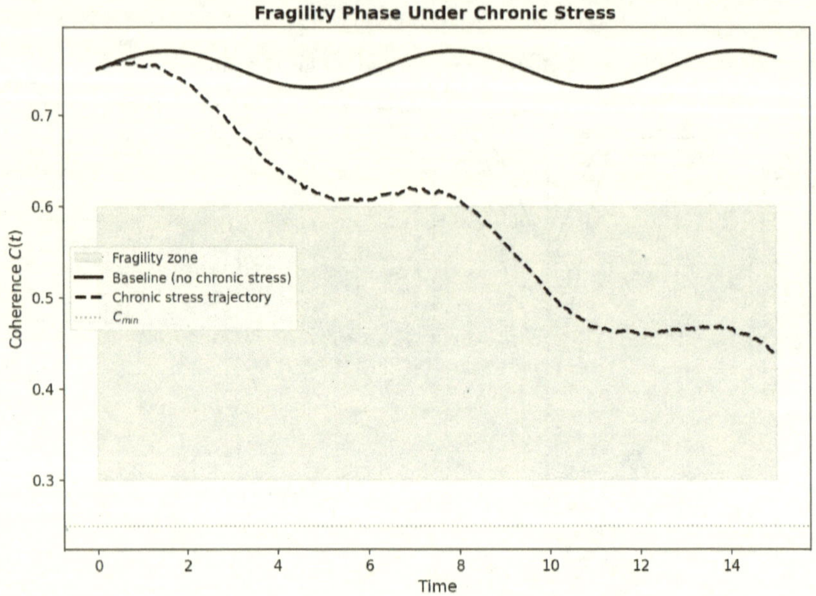


***Figure 4.*** *Fragility phase under chronic stress. Orange region:*

Integration declines while Adequacy remains temporarily stable — the system appears healthy but has lost resilience. Red region: Cascade collapse after Integration crosses the critical threshold.

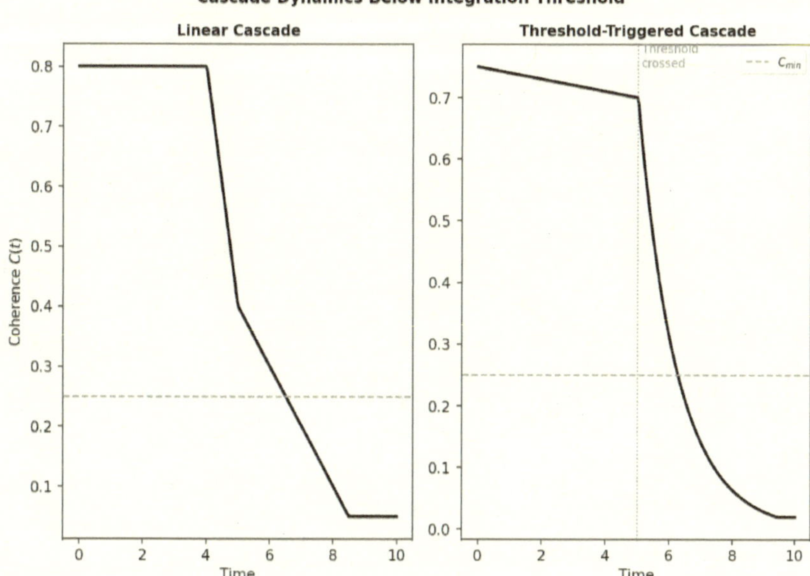


***Figure 5.*** *Cascade dynamics below integration threshold. Left: Linear*

scale showing gradual decay of Integration. Right: Logarithmic scale confirming approximately exponential collapse with fitted decay rate κ_eff ≈ 0.024.

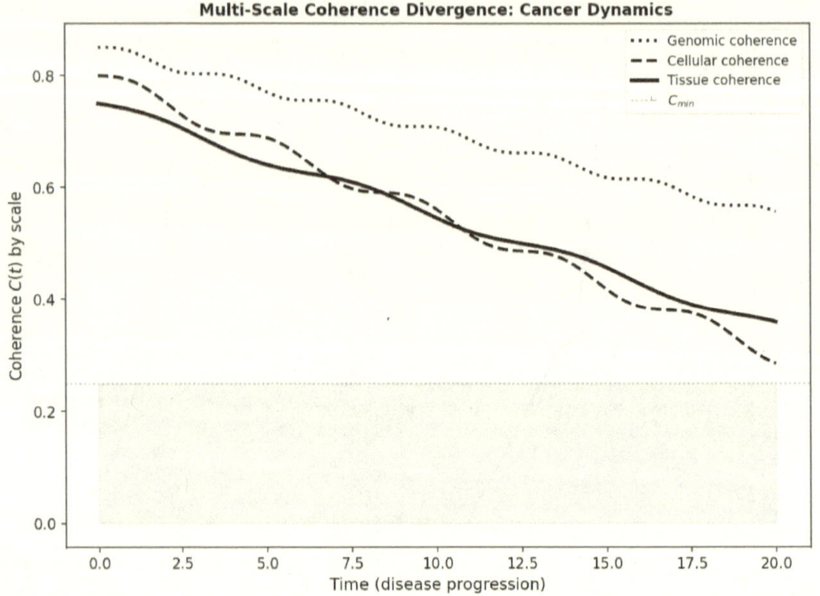


***Figure 6.*** *Multi-scale coherence divergence modeling cancer dynamics.*

After t=40, the cell begins local optimization: cell coherence rises while tissue coherence falls. This violates the Local—Global Coherence Principle — local gains that damage global integration are ultimately unsustainable.

This section has developed the mathematical framework: the coherence functional C(x) = A(x) · I(x) decomposing biological coherence into accessibility and integration, the constraint manifold K_t, coherence gradients, and the formal conditions for coherence collapse. The cancer model demonstrates the framework's analytical power: when a subsystem optimizes locally at the expense of global integration, it violates the Local—Global Coherence Principle and produces the characteristic divergence signature of malignancy.

# Section 3: Thermodynamic Foundations — The Cost and Possibility of Coherence

Living systems are thermodynamically open. They persist by continuously exchanging energy and matter with their environments, maintaining internal organization far from equilibrium. This feature distinguishes biological systems from static structures and places fundamental constraints on how life can exist, originate, and evolve. Understanding these constraints is essential before examining how coherence first emerged (Section 4) and how it is subsequently maintained (Sections V—IX).

## 3.1 The thermodynamic predicament

At thermodynamic equilibrium, systems minimize free energy and maximize entropy subject to external constraints. Living systems, by contrast, operate in regimes where equilibrium would correspond to death. Their defining challenge is not to reach equilibrium but to avoid it.

Schrödinger (1944) framed this insight as the problem of "negative entropy": organisms maintain internal order by importing free energy and exporting entropy to their surroundings. CU reframes this: entropy measures coherence rendered inaccessible at a given scale (CU-FP6), not coherence destroyed. Prigogine and Stengers (1984) formalized the conditions under which far-from-equilibrium systems can sustain organized structure through continuous energy dissipation, terming such configurations dissipative structures. More recently, England (2013, 2015) has shown that driven systems under certain conditions are statistically biased toward configurations that are good at dissipating energy — suggesting that the emergence of organized, energy-channeling structures is not thermodynamically anomalous but thermodynamically expected.

These results establish that physics does not forbid persistent far-from-equilibrium organization. The deeper question is why some such organizations become self-maintaining while most do not.

## 3.2 Coherence as structured dissipation

From the perspective developed in this paper, the energetic requirement of life reflects a constraint that goes beyond mere dissipation. Coherence is not a passive property of biological systems but an actively maintained one. Energy is expended not simply to perform work but to preserve the integration of system components across scales. Metabolism, in this sense, is not merely a source of fuel; it is the physical substrate of coherence maintenance.

This claim can be connected to the mathematical framework of Section 2. Recall that the coherence functional $C(x) = A(x) \cdot I(x)$ requires both adequacy (each constraint satisfied) and integration (constraints mutually supporting). The maintenance cost of coherence (§2.11) establishes that:

$$E\_maintain \geq \lambda \cdot C(x)$$

where λ represents the rate of entropic degradation and E_maintain is the minimum energy throughput required to sustain coherence at level C(x). This inequality captures a fundamental biological reality: coherence has a price, paid continuously through structured dissipation.

not all nonequilibrium structures are biologically meaningful. Hurricanes, convection cells, and chemical oscillations all dissipate energy and maintain transient organization, yet they do not preserve their own constraint structure across perturbation. What distinguishes living systems is that their internal dynamics are shaped by the requirement to remain within a narrow range of viable states. Energy dissipation is therefore structured — organized around viability constraints rather than merely driven by thermodynamic gradients.

## 3.3 Consequences for biological dynamics

This structured dissipation gives rise to characteristic biological behaviors: robustness to noise, rapid recovery from perturbation, and adaptive reconfiguration under stress. When coherence is challenged — by injury, environmental change, or internal fluctuation — biological systems do not simply decay. They activate compensatory processes that restore integration. These processes are energetically costly, yet they are favored because coherence loss carries existential consequences.

Thermodynamic constraints also explain why coherence failure is often abrupt rather than gradual. As systems approach critical thresholds, small perturbations can trigger cascading breakdowns — a phenomenon formalized in §2.9 as coherence collapse. This is observed empirically in phenomena ranging from metabolic collapse to organ failure to ecosystem tipping points. Once coherence drops below certain limits, recovery may become impossible despite continued energy availability. The system has exited its basin of repair.

## 3.4 The question thermodynamics raises but cannot answer

Seen through this lens, life can be understood as a continuous negotiation with thermodynamic reality. Biological systems persist by channeling energy flows in ways that preserve integrated organization, while remaining flexible enough to adapt to changing conditions. Coherence is neither free nor guaranteed. It is purchased moment by moment through structured dissipation.

But thermodynamics alone cannot explain why this negotiation ever began. Physics permits far-from-equilibrium organization. Dissipative structure theory describes conditions under which such organization can be sustained. Yet neither explains the transition from passive structure — organization that persists only while external conditions happen to be favorable — to active self-maintenance — organization that modifies its own boundary conditions to ensure its own continuation. That transition is the origin of life. The next section examines it directly.

## Section 4: Abiogenesis as a Coherence Phase Transition

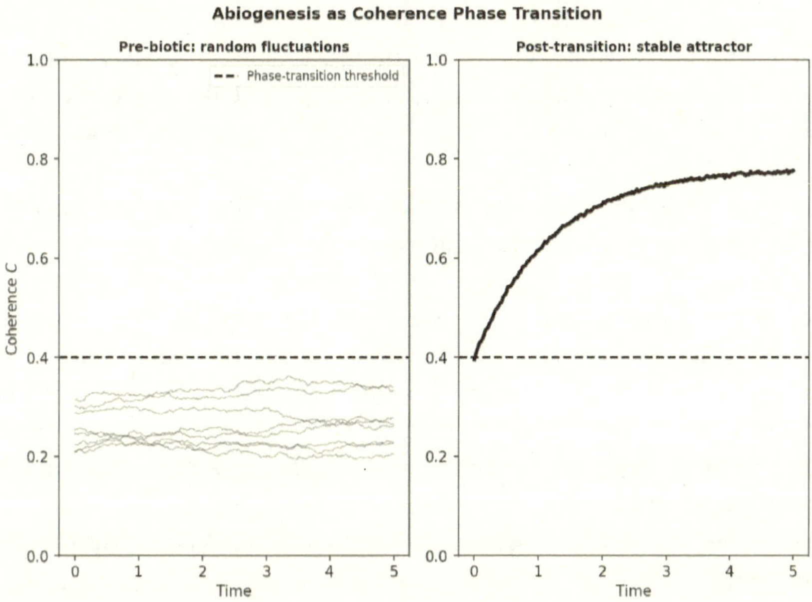


*Figure 7. Abiogenesis as a coherence phase transition. Left: The*

**recurrence dominance** criterion — the abiogenesis threshold is crossed when the probability of remaining in the living region L, given current membership, exceeds the probability of spontaneous entry from outside. Right: Regime transitions from equilibrium structure through pre-living complexity to biological coherence.

The origin of life remains one of the central open questions in biology. Traditional approaches divide into competing explanatory programs — RNA-world hypotheses, metabolism-first models, lipid-world scenarios, hydrothermal vent theories — each proposing a particular chemical pathway by which living systems first appeared. These programs have produced important empirical insights, yet they share a common limitation: they focus on which molecules or reactions came first while leaving largely implicit the question of why matter ever began organizing into self-maintaining systems rather than simply equilibrating.

Thermodynamics predicts that systems tend toward equilibrium. Life does the opposite: it establishes and maintains far-from-equilibrium organization indefinitely. The previous section established that living systems persist by channeling energy flows to preserve integrated organization. But this characterization describes what life does, not how it first became possible. The origin of life is not primarily a question about molecular sequencing. It is a question about the emergence of a new dynamical regime — one in which matter begins preserving its own constraint structure across time.

Within the coherence framework developed in this paper, abiogenesis admits a precise reformulation. Life is coherence that actively resists its own dissipation (Appendix C, §C.3.5). Abiogenesis is therefore the transition from passive coherence — structure that persists only so long as external conditions permit — to active coherence maintenance — structure that modifies its own boundary conditions to ensure its continued existence. This transition can be described at three complementary explanatory levels, each addressing a different question about the origin of life.

### *4.1 Lens A — The Minimal Dynamical Criterion: Recurrence Dominance*

We begin with a state-space description that makes no assumptions about specific chemistry.

Let the environment be a dynamical system over macrostates S. Define a subset $L \subset S$ as the set of proto-living states — configurations possessing organized constraint structure (autocatalytic closure, compartmentalization, or any other form of self-reinforcing organization).

Before life, organized states appear and disappear stochastically. A vortex forms and dissipates. A crystal grows and dissolves. The environment produces organized configurations occasionally, but their appearance at one time does not increase the probability of their appearance at the next. The system has no memory of its own organization.

Abiogenesis occurs when the system crosses a recurrence threshold:

$$P(s_{t+1} \in L \mid s_t \in L) > P(s_{t+1} \in L \mid s_t \notin L)$$

This inequality defines a transition in causal persistence — one with the character of a phase transition, in that the system's qualitative dynamical behavior changes sharply at the threshold. Before the transition, the probability of organized structure at the next time step is independent of whether organized structure exists now. After the transition, the presence of organized structure increases the probability of its own continuation. The structure has become a cause of its own recurrence.

Heuristically, this can be understood in information-theoretic terms: the system's own organization becomes a stronger predictor of its next state than the environmental dynamics alone. More precisely, using the framework of transfer entropy (Schreiber, 2000; see also Walker & Davies, 2013), the causal information flow from the system's current organization to its future state exceeds the information contributed by environmental forcing. At this point, the system is no longer merely a physical configuration subject to external dynamics. It has become a temporal object — an entity whose future depends on its own past in a way that is not reducible to the environmental dynamics that produced it.

This criterion is deliberately minimal. It specifies what must become true in any world where life exists, regardless of the particular chemistry, energy source, or molecular substrate involved. It does not explain how the transition occurs — that is the task of mechanistic models — but it identifies the dynamical condition that any such mechanism must produce.

Several features of this criterion deserve emphasis. First, the threshold is sharp: either the conditional probability exceeds the unconditional probability, or it does not. This makes abiogenesis a phase transition rather than a gradual accumulation. Second, the criterion is substrate-independent: it applies to any system in any medium, not only to carbon-based chemistry in aqueous solution. Third, it immediately explains why abiogenesis need not be astronomically improbable. The question is not whether a particular molecule can form by chance, but whether physics permits feedback-stabilized constraints. If it does — and thermodynamics does not forbid it — then recurrence dominance is a generic possibility wherever energy gradients and sufficient molecular diversity coexist.

### *4.2 Lens B — Mechanistic Realization: Autocatalytic Constraint Closure*

The dynamical criterion of the previous subsection does not specify which chemical processes can realize recurrence dominance. We now ask what kinds of systems cross the threshold.

The general requirement is closure under throughput. A set of reactions R over molecular species M forms a living precursor when three conditions hold simultaneously: each reaction is catalyzed by products of the network, the network collectively regenerates its own components, and environmental flux supplies energy and raw materials but not the organization itself.

Formally, let $x = (x_1, x_2, \ldots, x_n)$ represent concentrations of molecular species. The dynamics take the form:

$$dx/dt = F(x) + E$$

where F(x) captures internal reaction dynamics (including auto-catalytic and cross-catalytic terms) and E represents environmental throughput — the supply of energy-rich substrates and the removal of waste products.

Abiogenesis occurs when there exists a bounded region $\Omega$ in concentration space such that a system starting in $\Omega$ returns to $\Omega$ with high probability over biologically relevant timescales:

$$P(x(t+\tau) \in \Omega \mid x(t) \in \Omega) > 1 - \delta$$

for small $\delta$ and characteristic return time $\tau$, under continuous environmental throughput E. The condition is stochastic recurrence rather than strict invariance — real proto-living systems may be displaced from $\Omega$ by perturbation but reliably return, just as real organisms temporarily depart from homeostatic ranges during stress and recover. The system has formed a self-maintaining chemical manifold: not an equilibrium configuration, but a far-from-equilibrium attractor sustained by continuous energy throughput. It regenerates its organizational structure, not merely its molecular components (cf. Varela, Maturana & Uribe, 1974).

Within this framework, the familiar candidates for prebiotic chemistry become mechanistic instantiations of a single organizational principle:

Autocatalytic reaction networks provide the catalytic closure necessary for self-regeneration. When reaction diversity exceeds a critical density, closure becomes statistically likely (Hordijk & Steel, 2004) — a result established by Kauffman's work on collectively autocatalytic sets (Kauffman, 1993, 2000).

Compartment formation (proto-membranes, vesicles, mineral surfaces) provides the boundary conditions that concentrate reactants and prevent dissipation. Without compartmentalization, closure is possible in principle but unstable in practice.

Energy gradients (hydrothermal vents, photochemistry, redox interfaces; Wächtershäuser, 1988; Martin & Russell, 2007) provide the throughput E that sustains far-from-equilibrium organization. Without energy flow, any organized configuration decays to equilibrium.

These are not competing hypotheses about which came first. They are complementary requirements for realizing the recurrence threshold. Catalytic closure provides the self-reinforcing dynamics. Compartmentalization provides the boundary conditions. Energy gradients provide the thermodynamic substrate. Different environments may realize these requirements through different chemistries, but the organizational logic remains invariant.

This analysis clarifies a longstanding puzzle in origin-of-life research. Why do different experimental approaches — warm little ponds, alkaline vents, volcanic pools, ice eutectic phases — all produce partially life-like chemistry? The coherence framework predicts this convergence: recurrence dominance can be approached through multiple chemical routes because the threshold condition is organizational rather than compositional. The chemistry varies; the dynamical criterion does not.

### *4.3 Lens C — Organizational Meaning: Viability and the Birth of Identity*

The two previous subsections describe when abiogenesis occurs and how chemistry can realize it. This subsection addresses a deeper question: what does the transition mean organizationally, and why does the same dynamical structure reappear throughout biology?

Define a viability function V(s) representing the probability that the system remains within a constraint-preserving region of state space:

V(s) = P(system remains viable \| current state s)

Before abiogenesis, the system's future viability depends primarily on external conditions:

V(s_{t+1}) ≈ V(environment)

After abiogenesis, viability becomes self-referential:

V(s_{t+1}) = f(V(s_t))

The system has begun preserving its own future. This is the birth of biological identity in the precise sense developed in the mathematical framework (§2.8). The organism is not a collection of molecules; it is a persistent solution to a constraint equation. Its identity resides not in its material composition — which changes continuously — but in the continuity of its constraint structure across time.

This perspective reveals that abiogenesis, morphogenesis, and evolution are not separate biological mysteries but successive expressions of the same dynamical principle operating at different stability scales.

Abiogenesis establishes viability: matter first crosses the threshold at which organization becomes self-maintaining. Chemistry ceases to be merely reactive and begins preserving a region of state space against perturbation.

Once systems persist, differential persistence becomes possible. Some organizations maintain viability more reliably across environmental variation than others. Selection follows necessarily — not as an added mechanism but as the statistical consequence of unequal stability. Evolution begins at the moment persistence admits comparison across variants.

As evolutionary processes accumulate constraint, organisms eventually maintain not just chemical continuity but spatial and functional organization across scales. Morphogenesis extends viability preservation into geometry — the maintenance of position within a higher-dimensional viability space that includes anatomical configuration. Levin's regeneration experiments (§2.13) demonstrate this directly: a planarian cut in half regrows a head not by following local molecular instructions but by minimizing distance to a target configuration in morphological state space.

The relationship can be summarized:

Abiogenesis: viability emerges (persistence) Evolution: viability is compared across variants (refinement) Morphogenesis: viability is enforced within individual bodies (restoration)

Morphogenesis is thus abiogenesis running continuously. Every act of regeneration, every developmental sequence, every wound-healing process recapitulates the original transition from passive to active coherence maintenance — not historically, but dynamically. The organism is not built once and then maintained. It is continuously re-solved, moment by moment, as a constraint satisfaction problem.

This unification carries a further implication. If abiogenesis, evolution, and morphogenesis share a common dynamical structure, then understanding any one of them illuminates the others. The coherence framework developed in the preceding sections — viability constraints, coherence gradients, attractor dynamics, multi-scale integration —

applies not only to extant organisms but to the very process by which life first arose. Biology's three central mysteries become three faces of a single principle: the preservation of coherence across time.

## 4.4 Relation to Existing Origin-of-Life Frameworks

The coherence phase-transition account does not replace established origin-of-life theories. It provides a unifying criterion that explains why several seemingly different proposals converge on similar organizational structures.

Kauffman's work on collectively autocatalytic sets (1993, 2000) demonstrates that sufficiently rich chemical networks spontaneously form self-sustaining reaction cycles. In the present framework, these networks implement the mechanistic realization described in Lens B. Kauffman (1993) identifies a combinatorial threshold at which closure becomes statistically likely. The coherence framework interprets this threshold as one route to recurrence dominance: when catalytic network connectivity exceeds a critical density, the conditional probability P(s_{t+1} ∈ L \| s_t ∈ L) exceeds the unconditional probability. The significance of Kauffman's result is thereby elevated: it demonstrates that the coherence transition is statistically generic rather than chemically miraculous.

Metabolism-first models emphasize energy gradients and persistent reaction cycles prior to templated replication. These theories correctly identify the thermodynamic precondition for life: living systems must exist far from equilibrium, sustained by continuous energy throughput. In the present framework, this corresponds to the existence of a bounded viability region Ω maintained under environmental flux E. However, far-from-equilibrium existence is necessary but not sufficient. Hurricanes and flames dissipate energy yet do not preserve identity. What distinguishes living metabolism is not dissipation alone but constraint preservation across perturbations. Metabolism-first theories explain the energy source of coherence persistence; the recurrence criterion explains its organizational threshold.

RNA-world models propose that life began with self-replicating informational polymers capable of heredity and evolution (Szostak, Bartel & Luisi, 2001). Templated replication is indeed a powerful mechanism for increasing self-information transfer I(S_t; S_{t+1}), and it introduces the generational memory that enables evolution. However, replication alone cannot define life — crystals replicate structure but lack adaptive persistence. RNA-world mechanisms become biologically meaningful when embedded within a self-maintaining network. Thus replication provides a high-fidelity implementation of identity preservation but requires metabolic closure to stabilize viability.

Each major tradition therefore captures one dimension of the same transition. Autocatalytic set theory identifies the network closure condition. Metabolism-first models identify thermodynamic persistence. RNA-world models identify informational inheritance. The coherence framework proposes that these are complementary realizations of a single requirement: life begins when a system's organization becomes the dominant cause of its own continuation.

## 4.5 Falsifiable Predictions

If the origin of life corresponds to a coherence phase transition — the emergence of systems whose internal organization becomes the dominant cause of their own persistence — then the framework generates testable predictions distinct from traditional molecule-first hypotheses.

Network closure thresholds should predict life-like behavior better than specific chemistry. Across diverse chemical environments, life-like persistence should appear when reaction networks cross a critical closure density, regardless of molecular identity. Two different chemical systems with similar catalytic network connectivity should show similar emergence of self-maintaining behavior even if their molecules differ entirely. Conversely, a system rich in biologically relevant molecules but below closure threshold should fail to sustain organization. This predicts that the probability of proto-life emergence scales primarily with network topology rather than specific biomolecular composition.

Self-maintaining organization should precede reliable replication. The recurrence threshold can be crossed by metabolic closure alone, without templated replication. Laboratory systems should therefore exhibit bounded concentration regimes, recovery after perturbation, and environmental buffering prior to the appearance of Darwinian evolution. In other words, metabolism-like constraint preservation should experimentally precede heredity rather than depend on it. This provides a clear ordering test distinguishable from strict gene-first expectations.

Perturbation recovery should serve as the empirical signature of proto-life. The earliest living systems should be detectable not by reproduction but by homeostatic return dynamics. The operational test is straightforward: perturb a prebiotic chemical system (temperature spike, dilution, catalyst removal). If concentrations statistically return to a characteristic region of state space, the system has crossed the viability threshold. Formally, one should observe $P(s_{t+k} \in V \mid s_t \in V) > P(s_{t+k} \in V \mid s_t \notin V)$ for some bounded region V. This provides a measurable criterion distinguishing living from merely complex chemistry.

Convergent emergence should appear across independent experiments. Different laboratories recreating early-Earth conditions should observe convergence toward similar dynamical regimes even when molecular products differ. The framework predicts that life's universality appears as similarity of organization, not composition. Origin-of-life experiments may disagree chemically yet agree dynamically — a result currently treated as inconsistency but predicted here as expected.

Life-like persistence should be constructible in non-biological media. Provided recurrence dominance is achieved, artificial protocells need not resemble terrestrial biochemistry. Silicon-free, RNA-free, or even non--polymeric systems may cross the threshold. The first laboratory demonstration of long-term perturbation-recovering chemical organization would constitute a stronger confirmation of abiogenesis theory than the discovery of a specific replicating molecule.

The decisive empirical marker of abiogenesis, on this account (cf. Walker & Davies, 2013), is not replication, metabolism, or genetics individually, but the appearance of constraint-preserving dynamics measurable as return-to-viability after disturbance.

## 4.6 Summary: From Origin to Form

Abiogenesis is not a separate mystery from the biological phenomena examined in the remainder of this paper. It is their origin — the first instance of the dynamical principle that development, morphogenesis, and evolution subsequently elaborate.

Biology is unified not by shared molecules but by a shared dynamical requirement: systems must remain within a viable region of state space despite perturbation. The familiar distinctions among metabolism, heredity, and development reflect different regimes of the same constraint-preserving process rather than separate explanatory principles. The remainder of this paper examines how that process operates within individual lifetimes (Sections 5–9) and across evolutionary time (Section 10).

# Section 5: The Coherence Drive in Living Systems

Living systems do not merely persist by chance. Across scales and contexts, they exhibit systematic tendencies to preserve, restore, and reorganize integrated organization in response to disruption. These tendencies are evident in regulatory physiology, development, regeneration, and adaptive response to stress. While often described using diverse vocabularies—homeostasis, allostasis, robustness, resilience—these phenomena share a common structure: they function to maintain coherence over time. Here we introduce the concept of a coherence drive as a unifying biological descriptor. The term "drive" is used in a strictly functional sense. It does not imply intention, desire, subjective experience, or goal representation. Rather, it refers to the observable bias of living systems toward states that preserve integrated viability under constraint.

## 5.1 Coherence Drive versus Goal-Directedness

Biological systems are frequently described as "goal-directed," particularly in discussions of regulation and adaptation. However, such language can be misleading if interpreted cognitively. The coherence drive proposed here is not a psychological property and does not presuppose internal models or explicit optimization. Instead, it reflects the formal structure established in Section 2: the coherence functional $C(x)$ defines a landscape over state space, and the gradient $\nabla C(x)$ defines directions in which coherence increases or decreases. Living systems are structured such that departures from viable organization trigger dynamics that tend to move the system along $\nabla C$ — not because the system computes this gradient, but because configurations that move against it fail to persist. A thermostat regulates temperature without intending to do so, yet biological systems exhibit regulation far beyond simple feedback loops. The coherence drive captures this difference: it is the observable bias of biological dynamics toward higher $C(x)$, arising from the coupling between system dynamics and viability constraints rather than from representation or foresight.

## 5.2 Homeostasis, Allostasis, and Coherence Maintenance

Classical homeostasis describes the maintenance of internal variables within bounded ranges. While foundational, this framework is insufficient to capture the full scope of biological regulation. Many living systems anticipate, compensate, and reorganize in ways that cannot be explained by fixed setpoints alone. Allostasis extends this view by emphasizing predictive regulation and context sensitivity. In the language of

Section 2, homeostasis corresponds to maintaining individual constraint satisfactions $v_i(x)$ within acceptable bounds — preserving the adequacy term $A(x)$. Allostasis corresponds to adjusting which constraints are prioritized under changing conditions, preserving the integration term $I(x)$ even when individual setpoints shift. The coherence drive thus operates not by enforcing rigid stability but by enabling flexible regulation that preserves system-wide $C(x) = A(x) \cdot I(x)$, sometimes trading local constraint satisfaction for global integration.

## 5.3 Repair, Regeneration, and Reorganization

Perhaps the clearest expression of the coherence drive is biological repair. When tissues are damaged or disrupted, many organisms initiate processes that restore structure and function. These processes often reconstruct patterns rather than merely replacing parts. Regeneration illustrates this vividly. Organisms capable of regeneration do not simply regrow tissue; they restore coherent form. Limbs regenerate with appropriate orientation, organs reform in correct spatial relationships, and functional integration is reestablished across scales. In formal terms, perturbation displaces the system from its coherence attractor (§2.8). Repair is the trajectory back — guided by $\nabla C(x)$ toward the nearest viable basin. The energy cost of this return is the maintenance cost $E_{maintain}$ established in §3.2: coherence must be actively purchased through structured dissipation. Repair is expensive precisely because it requires restoring not just individual components (adequacy A) but their mutual support (integration I).

## 5.4 Failure Modes: Disease, Aging, and Death

The coherence drive also clarifies how and why biological systems fail. The collapse dynamics formalized in §2.9 describe the general pattern: when integration I(x) falls below a critical threshold I_crit, constraint violations propagate through the coupling structure rather than being absorbed, and recovery becomes impossible. Disease, aging, and death are instances of this general dynamic operating at different timescales.

Disease often manifests as partial coherence failure, where local processes become decoupled from global constraints. Cancer, examined in more detail in §6.4, involves cells that maintain local adequacy A while undermining organism-level integration I — a violation of the Local-Global Coherence Principle (§2.6). Aging reflects the progressive decline of repair capacity: the basin of repair (§2.8) shrinks over time as accumulated damage, regulatory drift, and loss of integration narrow the range of perturbations from which the system can recover. Death is the terminal failure mode: the irreversible loss of the constraint manifold K_t, as defined in §2.8.4.

## 5.5 Summary: coherence as the organizing principle of biological

regulation The coherence drive provides a unifying lens through which diverse biological phenomena can be understood. It explains why living systems actively regulate rather than passively persist, repair rather than merely endure damage, and reorganize rather than optimize narrowly defined functions. The coherence drive operates without invoking cognition, intention, or consciousness. It arises from the structural constraints imposed by living far from equilibrium and the necessity of maintaining integrated organization over time. With this foundation in place, we now turn to the multi-scale nature of coherence in biological systems, examining how integration is achieved and negotiated across nested levels of organization.

# Section 6: Multi-Scale Organization and Nested Coherence

Living systems are not organized at a single scale. From molecules to cells, tissues, organs, organisms, and ecosystems, biological coherence is distributed across nested levels of organization. Each level exhibits its own dynamics, constraints, and modes of failure, yet no level operates in isolation. The mathematical framework (§2.6) formalizes this as multi--scale coherence: global coherence C_global = (∏_s C^(s))^(1/S) · I_cross, where C^(s) is the coherence at scale s and I_cross measures whether coherence at one scale supports coherence at adjacent scales. This formulation enforces a crucial constraint — the Local-Global Coherence Principle — which states that high coherence at one scale that destroys coherence at another results in low C_global. This nested structure creates both power and vulnerability. It allows living systems to coordinate complex behavior and adapt to perturbation, but it also introduces tensions between local and global coherence that must be actively managed.

## 6.1 Cells as Semi-Autonomous Coherence-Maintaining Units

Cells are the fundamental units of life, yet they are not passive building blocks. Each cell maintains its own internal coherence through metabolic regulation, membrane integrity, and signaling networks. Cells actively sense their environment, respond to stress, and repair damage. However, cellular coherence is only conditionally autonomous. In multicellular organisms, individual cells must subordinate aspects of their local coherence to the requirements of the larger system. Differentiation, growth control, apoptosis, and migration are all mechanisms by which cellular behavior is constrained to preserve organism-level integration. This balance is nontrivial. Too much cellular autonomy undermines global coherence; too much global constraint suppresses adaptability. Healthy organisms maintain a dynamic equilibrium between these demands.

## 6.2 Tissues and Organs as Coherence-Coordinating Systems

At the tissue and organ level, coherence is maintained through coordinated signaling, mechanical coupling, and shared functional roles. Tissues are not mere collections of cells; they are structured ensembles that enforce spatial patterning, functional specialization, and collective response to perturbation. Developmental patterning, for example, relies on long-range coordination mechanisms that ensure cells adopt appropriate identities relative to one another. These mechanisms constrain local cellular dynamics so that global form emerges reliably despite noise

and variation. Similarly, organs integrate multiple tissue types into functional units that contribute to organism-level viability. Disruption at this scale often manifests as loss of coordination rather than failure of individual components.

## 6.3 Organism-Level Coherence and Control

The organism represents a higher-order coherence regime in which multiple subsystems are integrated into a unified, persistent entity. Nervous systems, endocrine signaling, immune surveillance, and circulatory networks all contribute to this integration. Organism-level coherence is not achieved by central control alone. While nervous systems play a significant role in many species, coherence is also maintained through distributed processes such as bioelectric signaling, chemical gradients, and mechanical feedback. This distributed control architecture allows organisms to remain robust in the face of local damage. When one subsystem fails, others can often compensate, at least temporarily, preserving overall viability.

## 6.4 Local versus Global Coherence: Tension and Pathology

The nested nature of biological organization creates inherent tensions between local and global coherence. These tensions are not accidental; they are a direct consequence of multi-scale integration, and the Local-Global Coherence Principle predicts exactly where pathology should appear: at points where C^(local) increases while I_cross decreases. Cancer provides a paradigmatic example. Cancerous cells often exhibit enhanced local coherence: they regulate metabolism effectively, proliferate robustly, and resist apoptosis. Their scale-specific coherence C^(cell) may be high. Yet I_cross — the cross-scale integration that couples cellular behavior to organism-level constraints — is degraded. The result is declining C_global despite rising C^(cell): the defining signature of a multi-scale coherence violation. From this perspective, cancer is not simply uncontrolled growth. It is a breakdown in cross-scale coherence enforcement. This reframing generates a testable prediction: cancer normalization therapies that restore I_cross (such as bioelectric reprogramming of tissue-level signaling) should be effective even without eliminating the locally coherent cancer cells themselves — a prediction consistent with Levin's experimental results on cancer normalization through bioelectric modulation (§2.13.4).

## 6.5 Immune Systems as Coherence Boundary Enforcement

Immune systems play a critical role in maintaining coherence across scales. They identify and respond to entities — pathogens, damaged cells, aberrant growth — that threaten system integration. Rather than functioning solely as defense mechanisms, immune system (an instance of internal error sensitivity, CU-V3)s can be understood as coherence boundary managers: they distinguish between components that can be integrated into the organismal whole and those that cannot. In formal terms, the immune system enforces the boundary of the viable region in state space, identifying states or components whose inclusion would reduce C_global. Failures of immune regulation illustrate this role clearly. Autoimmune disorders reflect excessive boundary enforcement — the system excludes components that should be integrated. Immune suppression permits local incoherence to proliferate — the boundary is not enforced, allowing threats to organism-level integration to persist. Chronic inflammation represents misaligned coherence signaling — the boundary management process itself consumes resources without resolving the underlying integration failure.

## 6.6 Summary

Biological coherence is not localized at any single level of organization. It emerges from the interaction of processes operating across nested scales, each with its own dynamics and constraints. Living systems persist by continuously negotiating the tension between local autonomy and global integration. Health reflects successful coordination across scales; pathology reflects breakdowns in that coordination. This multi-scale perspective sets the stage for

understanding how intelligence-like behavior can emerge without cognition. In the next section, we examine how embedded biological systems navigate coherence landscapes through real-time interaction with their environments.

# Section 7: Development, Morphogenesis, and Repair

Developmental biology confronts a central puzzle: how reliable form and function emerge from components that are noisy, variable, and frequently perturbed. Across species, organisms develop with remarkable consistency despite genetic variation, environmental fluctuation, and physical disruption. Even more strikingly, many organisms can repair or regenerate complex structures after damage, restoring appropriate form and integration rather than merely replacing lost material. These phenomena challenge purely local or feedforward explanations. They suggest that biological systems possess mechanisms for evaluating global structure and correcting deviations from it. From the perspective developed here, development, morphogenesis, and repair are expressions of coherence-seeking dynamics operating within constrained biological state spaces.

7.1 Development as coherence-seeking, not program execution

Development is often described metaphorically as the execution of a genetic program. While genes play an indispensable role, this metaphor is insufficient to explain the robustness and flexibility observed in real organisms. Developmental outcomes are not rigidly specified in advance; they are dynamically achieved. Experimental perturbations reveal this clearly. When embryos are physically rearranged, partially ablated, or chemically perturbed, development often proceeds toward normal form. Cells change fate, reorganize spatial relationships, and compensate for missing or altered signals. Such behavior indicates that development is guided by global constraints rather than by local instructions alone. In coherence terms, development can be understood as movement toward stable attractors in morphogenetic state space (§2.8). The coherence functional C(x) defines the landscape; genetic and molecular mechanisms shape its topology. But the system actively navigates toward viable configurations — regions where $C(x) > C\_min$ and $\nabla C$ points inward — even when typical developmental pathways are disrupted. This is why embryos subjected to radical perturbation often produce normal organisms: the attractor, not the pathway, determines the outcome.

## 7.2 Long-Range Coordination and Pattern Integrity

A key feature of morphogenesis is long-range coordination. Cells must not only differentiate appropriately but do so in relation to the positions, states, and fates of distant neighbors. Chemical gradients, mechanical forces, and bioelectric signals all contribute to this coordination. Bioelectric signaling, in particular, has emerged as a powerful regulator of large-scale patterning (Levin, 2014, 2021). Spatial distributions of membrane potentials and ion flows encode information about tissue identity, orientation, and boundaries. Disruptions to these patterns can lead to dramatic changes in morphology, while targeted interventions can induce controlled pattern transformations. These observations suggest that global pattern information is actively maintained and referenced during development and repair. Local cellular dynamics are constrained by higher-order organizational signals that preserve coherence across spatial scales.

## 7.3 Regeneration as Restoration of Coherent Form

Regeneration provides one of the clearest demonstrations that biological systems are oriented toward restoring integrated organization rather than merely replacing parts. In regenerating organisms, tissues reconstruct appropriate structures even when damage is severe or atypical. Limbs regenerate with correct orientation, organs reform with proper connectivity, and overall body plans are reestablished. These outcomes are not trivial consequences of local growth rules. They require coordination across tissues and the ability to evaluate whether form has been successfully restored. From a coherence perspective, regeneration corresponds to re-entry into the coherence attractor after displacement — the system follows $\nabla C$ through morphogenetic state space, not retracing a fixed developmental script but reorganizing until $C(x)$ exceeds the viability threshold. The target is not a stored template but an attractor: a self-stabilizing region of state space that the system's own dynamics tend to restore.

## 7.4 Robustness, Plasticity, and Error Correction

Developmental and regenerative systems exhibit a balance between robustness and plasticity. They reliably produce functional forms while remaining flexible enough to adapt to perturbation. This balance is difficult to explain using purely local or linear mechanisms. Error correction plays a central role. When patterning errors occur, biological systems often detect and correct them. Misplaced structures can be remodeled, excess tissue can be removed, and missing elements can be regenerated. These processes imply the existence of global coherence criteria that guide correction — formally, the system detects that C(x) has declined or that specific constraint satisfactions v_i(x) have fallen below threshold, and activates dynamics that restore them. Such criteria need not be explicit representations. They are implemented through the same distributed signaling, feedback loops, and constraint coupling that the integration measure I(x) quantifies (§2.5).

## 7.5 Morphogenesis as Continuous Abiogenesis

The abiogenesis analysis of Section 4 reveals a structural connection between the origin of life and morphogenesis that deepens the treatment of both phenomena.

Recall the abiogenesis criterion: life begins when a system's organization becomes the dominant cause of its own continuation. Morphogenesis, on this view, is the same principle operating within an established organism at a higher level of organization. Where abiogenesis establishes the first self-maintaining chemical attractor, morphogenesis maintains a specific spatial and functional configuration within an already-living system.

The parallel is precise. At the origin of life, matter first stabilized a pattern — a self-maintaining chemical organization that caused its own recurrence. In morphogenesis, the organism stabilizes a form — a body plan that is actively restored after perturbation. The abiogenesis threshold asks whether $P(L \to L) > P(\neg L \to L)$. Morphogenesis asks the analogous question at a higher scale: whether the organism's developmental dynamics reliably restore a target morphology after disturbance.

Levin's experimental program (§2.13) demonstrates this connection empirically. When a planarian is cut in half, the cells do not locally know what to build. Instead, the organism behaves like a system minimizing distance to a target configuration in morphological state space:

min D(current form, target form)

This is structurally identical to the abiogenesis transition from random chemistry to self-maintaining attractor. The only difference is that the attractor now exists in a higher-dimensional state space that includes anatomical configuration.

Regeneration is therefore not a strange add-on to biology. It is the same dynamical principle that produced life in the first place, operating at a higher level of organization. Every wound-healing process, every developmental sequence, every tissue homeostasis event recapitulates the original transition from passive to active coherence maintenance — not historically, but dynamically. A salamander limb is closer to a standing wave than a machine. Destroy part of the wave and it reappears — because what persists is not the material but the dynamical process that maintains the pattern.

The connection to Section 4 is therefore direct: morphogenesis is abiogenesis running continuously. Regeneration is the organism re-crossing the same viability threshold that matter first crossed at the origin of life.

## 7.6 Summary

Development, morphogenesis, and repair are not best understood as the execution of prespecified plans. They are better understood as processes through which biological systems navigate constrained spaces of viable form. Energy, signaling, and genetic mechanisms shape these spaces, but coherence provides the organizing principle that explains robustness, flexibility, and adaptive correction. The system persists not by rigid adherence to a script, but by maintaining integration in the face of uncertainty. This interpretation prepares the ground for a broader claim. If development and repair involve real-time navigation of coherence landscapes, then intelligencelike behavior need not be confined to brains or nervous systems. In the next section, we examine how such behavior emerges naturally in embedded biological systems.

# Section 8: Embedded Intelligence and Coherence-Gradient Navigation

The preceding sections have documented intelligence-like behavior in systems lacking brains, neurons, or representational machinery: embryos that recover normal form after radical perturbation, tissues that regenerate complex structures, organisms that solve problems outside their evolutionary history. This section argues that such behavior is not anomalous but expected once we take seriously the formal structure established in Section 2. The coherence functional C(x) defines a structured landscape over state space. The gradient ∇C(x) provides directionality. Viability constraints bound the space of acceptable trajectories. A system embedded in this landscape and subject to these constraints will exhibit intelligence-like behavior — adaptive, context-sensitive, error-correcting — without requiring cognition, representation, or foresight.

## 8.1 Intelligence without Cognition

If intelligence is defined narrowly as symbolic reasoning or conscious deliberation, then most biological systems are excluded by definition. Yet cells adjust to stress, tissues repair damage, and organisms reorganize development in response to perturbation — behaviors involving sensing, integration, and action that do not require explicit representations or foresight. In this framework, intelligence is understood functionally: a system behaves intelligently insofar as it reliably maintains C(x) above viability thresholds when confronted with disruption. This definition does not collapse intelligence into mere reactivity. What distinguishes intelligent response from simple reaction is the structured, context-sensitive character of the system's trajectory through state space — it navigates toward coherence rather than merely responding to local stimuli.

## 8.2 Embeddedness and Constraint-Driven Behavior

A defining feature of biological intelligence is embeddedness. Living systems are not detached problem solvers operating in abstract spaces; they are physically embedded in environments that impose energetic, spatial, and temporal constraints. This embeddedness matters because it shapes the structure of the coherence landscape the system must navigate. Environmental pressures deform the space of viable states, while internal organization determines how the system can respond. Intelligence emerges from the interaction between these factors. From this perspective, adaptive behavior does not require the system to "know" what to do in advance. It only requires the capacity to respond differentially to perturbations in ways that preserve integration. Coherence gradients provide directionality without representation.

## 8.3 Coherence-Gradient Navigation

The coherence functional C(x) defines a landscape over biological state space (§2.7). The gradient ∇C(x) specifies, at each point, the direction in which coherence increases most steeply. The landscape is structured: viable regions form attractors with inward-pointing gradients (§2.8), while incoherent states are dynamically unstable. The system's dynamics dx/dt = F(x, e, t) need not explicitly compute ∇C. But configurations that move against the gradient tend to violate viability constraints and are eliminated — either the system corrects or it fails. The result is an effective bias toward gradient-following without explicit optimization.

This is the core mechanism of embedded biological intelligence. When perturbations displace the system, intrinsic dynamics guided by ∇C tend to restore coherence. The system does not search randomly (which would be too slow), nor does it execute precomputed solutions (which would be too rigid). Instead, it reorganizes along the coherence gradient until integration is restored. The quality of the response depends on the structure of the landscape — specifically, on the width of the basin of repair and the smoothness of the gradient field within it.

## 8.4 Distributed Problem Solving across Scales

Because coherence is maintained across nested scales, problem solving in biological systems is inherently distributed. Cells, tissues, and organs each contribute to coherence maintenance, often without centralized control. For example, during regeneration, local cellular responses interact

with global pattern constraints to restore form. No single component "knows" the final outcome, yet coordinated behavior emerges reliably.

This distributed intelligence is robust precisely because it does not depend on any single locus of control. Such systems are capable of responding to problems they have never encountered before, as long as those problems can be resolved through reorganization within the space of viable configurations.

## 8.5 Summary

Embedded biological systems exhibit intelligence-like behavior because they are forced to navigate coherence landscapes in order to persist. This navigation is guided by constraint, not cognition; by integration, not representation. Understanding intelligence in this way dissolves the sharp boundary between "simple" biological regulation and "complex" adaptive behavior. It reveals a continuum of coherence-driven processes operating across living systems. This perspective prepares us to address a striking empirical fact: organisms can solve novel problems that lie outside their evolutionary history. The next section examines such cases directly, illustrating how coherence-gradient navigation enables genuine biological novelty.

# Section 9: Novel Problem Solving Without Evolutionary Precedent

A central assumption in much of evolutionary biology is that adaptive solutions are shaped by prior selective history. Traits that improve survival and reproduction are retained; those that do not are eliminated. While this framework explains population-level adaptation over generational timescales, it does not fully account for a growing body of evidence showing that individual organisms can solve problems they have never encountered before, and for which no direct evolutionary precedent exists. These cases do not merely involve the deployment of preexisting mechanisms in familiar contexts. Instead, they reveal the capacity of biological systems to generate genuinely novel solutions in real time. Understanding this capacity requires moving beyond evolution alone and examining the coherence dynamics operating within individual organisms.

***9.1 The limits of evolutionary explanation at the organismal timescale***

Natural selection operates across populations and generations. Its explanatory power lies in shaping developmental pathways, regulatory architectures, and material constraints. However, selection cannot directly explain adaptive responses that arise within a single lifetime when environmental challenges fall outside historical conditions. If an organism encounters a perturbation that has no direct analog in its evolutionary past, disrupts canonical developmental or physiological pathways, and demands rapid reorganization to survive, then the organism must rely on mechanisms other than stored genetic solutions. In such cases, the system must construct responses dynamically, using whatever degrees of freedom remain available.

***9.2 Empirical case: adaptive reorganization in novel toxic environments***

Experimental work in regenerative organisms provides clear illustrations of this phenomenon. In one class of experiments, planarian flatworms were placed in environments containing substances that disrupt normal bioelectric signaling, such as barium ions. Under these conditions, standard morphogenetic processes fail: many organisms die, and those that survive cannot form canonical head structures using their usual developmental pathways. Remarkably, some planaria respond by regenerating heads with radically altered anatomical and physiological configurations that nonetheless allow survival in the toxic environment. These novel morphologies are not typical variants observed in nature, nor are they encoded as alternative developmental programs in the genome. They emerge only under the imposed constraints. The organisms have no evolutionary history of living in such environments, the solutions arise within a single lifetime, and the resulting forms are functionally integrated and viable. These outcomes cannot be explained as the activation of latent genetic programs alone. They reflect real-time problem solving at the level of the whole organism.

## 9.3 Coherence Landscapes and Constrained Novelty

From the perspective developed in this paper, these results are not anomalous. They are a direct consequence of coherence-driven dynamics. The imposed environment radically reshapes the organism's coherence landscape. Formally, the environmental input e enters the dynamics $dx/dt = F(x, e, t)$, deforming the coherence functional $C(x)$ so that canonical morphologies no longer correspond to viable attractors — $C(x_{canonical})$ drops below $C_{min}$ under the new conditions.

The system is now displaced from its historical attractor with no gradient path back to it. But the coherence landscape is not featureless. Other regions of state space may satisfy $C(x) > C_{min}$ under the altered constraints. The system's dynamics, guided by $\nabla C$ in the deformed landscape, tend to move it toward these alternative viable regions. The novelty of the resulting solution does not arise from random exploration — which would be astronomically unlikely to find a viable configuration in a high-dimensional state space. It arises from guided navigation within a structured landscape. The coherence gradient provides directionality; viability constraints provide boundaries; and the system's existing regulatory architecture provides the degrees of freedom through which reorganization can occur.

This analysis yields a specific prediction: the probability of successful novel adaptation should correlate with the richness of the organism's regulatory architecture (which determines how many degrees of freedom are available for reorganization) and the smoothness of the coherence landscape (which determines whether gradient-following can reach alternative viable regions). Organisms with more flexible developmental systems should solve novel problems more reliably — a prediction consistent with the observation that organisms with strong regenerative capacity also tend to exhibit greater developmental plasticity.

## 9.4 Novelty without Foresight or Representation

this form of problem solving does not require cognition, planning, or internal models. The organism does not represent the challenge it faces or calculate an optimal response. Instead, adaptive novelty emerges from the interaction between the organism's existing regulatory architecture, the constraints imposed by the environment, and the requirement to maintain coherence over time. This explains how systems can generate solutions that are both novel and functional without invoking learning in the cognitive sense or foresight in the evolutionary sense.

## 9.5 Implications for Understanding Adaptation

These observations support a claim that goes beyond standard evolutionary biology. Evolution does not merely select for specific traits; it selects for systems capable of solving problems evolution itself is too slow to solve. Genomes, developmental pathways, and regulatory networks shape the coherence landscape — they determine the topology of viable regions, the structure of attractor basins, and the degrees of freedom available for reorganization. But within that landscape, organisms actively navigate to construct solutions in real time.

This creates a feedback loop across timescales. Within a lifetime, organisms navigate coherence landscapes to solve immediate problems. Across generations, evolution shapes those landscapes by selecting for architectures that navigate well. The result is that evolutionary lineages accumulate not just adaptive traits but adaptive capacity — the ability to find novel solutions under novel constraints. This capacity is not a single trait but a property of the coherence landscape itself: its dimensionality, its smoothness, and the accessibility of alternative viable regions. Evolution selects for landscapes that are navigable, not merely for positions within them.

## 9.6 Summary

Biological novelty is not confined to mutation and selection across generations. It also arises through coherence-driven reorganization within individual lifetimes. Organisms can solve genuinely new problems by navigating constrained spaces of viable configurations, even when standard developmental pathways are unavailable. This capacity reveals a deeper structure underlying biological adaptability—one that bridges development, repair, and evolution without invoking cognition or chance alone. In the next section, we extend this perspective across generational timescales, reinterpreting evolution itself as a process shaped by coherence flow rather than random search.

# Section 10: Evolution as Coherence Flow Across Generations

Evolutionary theory has been remarkably successful in explaining the diversification and adaptation of life. Variation, inheritance, and differential reproduction account for a vast range of biological phenomena. Yet standard evolutionary explanations often leave implicit a deeper question: why adaptive solutions cluster so strongly around particular forms, structures, and strategies rather than exploring biological possibility space uniformly. From the perspective developed here, evolution is not best understood as a blind search through an unconstrained space of forms. Instead, it is a process shaped by coherence constraints that channel variation and stabilize viable configurations across generations. Evolutionary dynamics unfold within structured landscapes defined by the requirements of integrated biological organization.

## 10.1 Randomness in Variation, Structure in Outcomes

Mutations arise stochastically with respect to fitness. Developmental noise, recombination, and environmental fluctuations introduce variability at multiple levels. In this sense, evolutionary variation is genuinely random. However, evolutionary outcomes are strikingly non-random. Certain solutions recur across independent lineages: eyes, bilateral symmetry, centralized nervous systems, segmented bodies, and similar metabolic pathways emerge repeatedly. These patterns suggest that biological possibility space is highly constrained. Within the coherence framework, this asymmetry is expected. While variation may be random, persistence is not. Only configurations that maintain coherence across developmental, physiological, and ecological scales can endure. As a result, evolutionary trajectories are biased toward regions of state space where coherence can be sustained.

## 10.2 Fitness as Coherence Persistence

Fitness is often defined operationally as reproductive success. While useful, this definition obscures the mechanisms by which such success is achieved. Reproductive success requires the maintenance of organismal coherence long enough to develop, survive, and reproduce in a given environment. From this perspective, fitness can be reinterpreted as the capacity of a lineage to preserve coherence across time and scale. Traits that enhance robustness, repair, adaptability, and integration contribute to fitness not because they are optimal in isolation, but because they support persistent organization under constraint. This reinterpretation aligns with observations that: — robustness often matters more than peak efficiency, — redundant or degenerate systems enhance survival, — and organisms that tolerate variability frequently outcompete those optimized for narrow conditions.

## 10.3 Canalization, Reuse, and Evolutionary Memory

Evolutionary systems exhibit canalization: developmental outcomes remain stable despite genetic and environmental variation. Once established, successful forms are reused, modified, and elaborated rather than discarded. This phenomenon can be understood as the stabilization of deep coherence basins in evolutionary state space. Developmental pathways that reliably produce viable organisms carve persistent channels through which future variation flows. New traits are layered onto existing structures rather than constructed de novo. In this sense, evolution exhibits memory. Past coherence solutions constrain future possibilities, not through explicit encoding alone, but through the structural organization of developmental and regulatory systems.

## 10.4 Convergent evolution as evidence of constrained landscapes

Convergent evolution provides some of the strongest evidence for structured coherence landscapes. Independent lineages repeatedly arrive at similar solutions when faced with comparable constraints. These solutions are not identical in detail, but they occupy analogous regions of biological state space. Within a coherence framework, convergence reflects the fact that only certain configurations can sustain integrated function under given conditions. When organisms explore similar regions of environmental constraint, they are drawn toward similar coherence-preserving solutions. This does not diminish the role of contingency in evolution. Instead, it clarifies its boundaries. History matters, but it unfolds within constrained possibility spaces.

## 10.5 Major Evolutionary Transitions as Coherence Reorganization

Major transitions in evolution—such as the emergence of multicellularity, sexual reproduction, eusociality, and complex nervous systems—can be understood as shifts in coherence scale. These transitions involve the formation of new levels of integration, with corresponding new failure modes and regulatory challenges. Such transitions are costly and fragile. They succeed only

when new mechanisms of coherence maintenance emerge to manage conflicts between subunits. For example: — multicellularity requires suppression of cellular autonomy, — social systems require enforcement of cooperation, — neural systems require integration of distributed signals. Once established, these new coherence regimes open expanded spaces of adaptive possibility.

## 10.6 Selection for Problem-Solving Capacity

The organism-level phenomena described earlier have direct evolutionary implications. Systems capable of navigating coherence landscapes within a lifetime gain a selective advantage. They can respond to novel challenges more rapidly than evolution alone would permit. Over time, evolution favors architectures that support such flexibility: regulatory networks, developmental plasticity, modular organization, and repair mechanisms. Selection thus operates not only on specific traits, but on the capacity to generate adaptive responses under constraint. Evolution, in this view, selects for systems that can solve problems evolution itself is too slow to solve.

## 10.7 Summary

Evolutionary dynamics unfold within structured landscapes defined by coherence constraints. Variation supplies exploration; coherence determines persistence. The result is neither blind randomness nor directed design, but constrained flow through biological possibility space. This perspective preserves the core insights of evolutionary theory while clarifying why adaptive solutions are both diverse and recurrent. Evolution shapes the terrain; organisms traverse it; coherence determines what endures. Having established this framework across individual and generational timescales, we now turn to a minimal account of biological epistemology—what it means, if anything, for organisms to "know" or "sense" their world within coherence-driven dynamics.

# Section 11: Minimal Biological Epistemology

Biological systems continuously interact with their environments. They sense changes, respond to perturbations, and adjust internal processes to preserve viability. These interactions invite epistemic language—terms such as "information," "knowledge," and "error"—yet such language risks importing cognitive assumptions that are unwarranted at the biological level. This section develops a minimal biological epistemology that remains grounded in physiology and regulation rather than representation or consciousness. The goal is not to claim that organisms possess beliefs or models, but to clarify what kind of world-directed sensitivity is required for coherence maintenance.

## 11.1 Sensitivity without Representation

At the most basic level, biological systems must be sensitive to relevant environmental variables. Cells respond to nutrient availability, toxins, temperature, and mechanical stress. These responses do not require internal representations of the environment; they require only reliable coupling between external conditions and internal dynamics. In this sense, biological "knowing" is not a matter of encoding facts about the world. It is a matter of differential responsiveness: the system behaves differently in different conditions in ways that affect its coherence. Such sensitivity is ubiquitous in living systems and does not imply cognition. It reflects the fact that coherence cannot be maintained without continual engagement with the environment.

## 11.2 Information as Coherence-Relevant Difference

Information is often defined abstractly as reduction of uncertainty or transmission of signals. In biological contexts, a more constrained notion is required. Not all differences matter to a living system; only those differences that affect coherence are biologically relevant. From this perspective, information can be understood as coherence-relevant difference. A signal carries information for a system if responding to it alters the system's ability to maintain integrated organization. This definition avoids semantic commitments while preserving explanatory power. It aligns with empirical practice, where biological signals are identified by their functional consequences rather than by representational content.

## 11.3 Error, Correction, and Normativity

Biological regulation involves error detection and correction. Deviations from viable ranges trigger compensatory responses. These errors are defined relative to the system's own coherence constraints, not to externally imposed goals. Normativity enters biology not through intention, but through viability. States that undermine coherence are "wrong" for the system in a functional sense, regardless of whether the system represents them as such. This intrinsic normativity explains why biological systems can correct themselves without awareness. Error correction is a consequence of constraint satisfaction, not evaluation.

## 11.4 Learning and Plasticity as Landscape Reshaping

Some biological systems exhibit learning and plasticity: past interactions alter future responses. Within the coherence framework, learning can be understood as reshaping the coherence landscape itself. Regulatory pathways are modified so that certain responses become more likely

or more effective under recurring conditions. This process does not require symbolic memory. Structural changes—synaptic modification, epigenetic regulation, tissue remodeling—encode history directly into the system's dynamics. Learning, in this sense, increases the system's ability to maintain coherence across a broader range of conditions.

## 11.5 Summary

Minimal biological epistemology requires no appeal to belief, representation, or consciousness. It requires only that systems be structured such that coherence-relevant differences in the environment can influence internal dynamics. This framing preserves the explanatory utility of informational language while keeping biological claims firmly grounded. It also prepares the ground for later comparisons with cognitive and artificial systems, where representational and semantic commitments may or may not be appropriate. With this biological foundation in place, we now turn to a brief contrast case. Artificial systems provide a useful foil, clarifying which features of coherence maintenance are intrinsic to living systems and which can be externally supplied.

# Section 12: Artificial Systems as a Contrast Case

Artificial systems provide a useful contrast for understanding biological coherence. Like living systems, artificial systems can exhibit complex behavior, process information, and respond to environmental inputs. However, the way coherence is achieved and maintained in artificial systems differs fundamentally from that of biological organisms. This contrast helps clarify which features of coherence-driven dynamics are intrinsic to life and which can be externally imposed.

## 12.1 Externalized versus Internalized Coherence Costs

Biological systems internalize the costs of maintaining coherence. Energy expenditure, repair, regulation, and failure all occur within the system itself. When coherence collapses, the organism ceases to function as a living entity. Artificial systems, by contrast, typically externalize coherence costs. Their stability is maintained through: external power supplies, — human-designed architectures, — monitoring and intervention, — and environmental control. When an artificial system fails, its coherence can often be restored externally without intrinsic reorganization. The system does not bear the existential consequences of incoherence in the way living systems do.

## 12.2 Constraint Enforcement in Artificial Systems

In biological systems, coherence constraints are enforced intrinsically through multi-scale coupling and energetic limitations. In artificial systems, constraints are largely imposed by design. Algorithms, architectures, and training regimes define the permissible space of system behavior. While artificial systems may exhibit adaptive dynamics within these spaces, the coherence of the

system as a whole is not self-maintaining. It depends on continued alignment between system behavior and external scaffolding. This distinction explains why artificial systems can display impressive local performance without exhibiting the same kinds of global robustness, repair, or self-preservation observed in biological organisms.

## 12.3 Implications for Comparison

The contrast between biological and artificial systems is not a matter of complexity or intelligence alone. It is a matter of where coherence resides and who pays its costs. Biological systems are forced to navigate coherence landscapes because failure carries irreversible consequences. Artificial systems operate within coherence landscapes engineered and maintained by others. Recognizing this distinction prevents both over--ascription and under-ascription of biological properties to artificial systems. It also clarifies why biological coherence provides such a strong empirical foundation for broader theoretical claims.

## 12.4 Summary

Artificial systems can illuminate aspects of coherence dynamics, but they do not replace biology as the primary empirical domain in which coherence is intrinsic rather than imposed. Understanding life requires understanding systems that must maintain their own integration under constraint. This contrast sharpens the biological claims developed in this paper and prepares the ground for a return to empirical rigor. In the next section, we outline testable predictions and experimental directions that follow directly from the coherence-based framework presented here.

# Section 13: Predictions and Experimental Program

The coherence-based framework developed in this paper makes specific, testable predictions about biological systems across scales. These predictions are not post hoc reinterpretations of existing data; they arise directly from treating coherence as a dynamical constraint on living systems. The framework also suggests experimental strategies for identifying and manipulating the mechanisms by which coherence is maintained, lost, and restored. This section outlines several classes of predictions and corresponding experimental approaches.

## 13.1 Coherence Gradients Are Experimentally Manipulable

Prediction: If biological systems navigate coherence landscapes, then targeted perturbations should reshape these landscapes in predictable ways, altering developmental, regenerative, or adaptive outcomes. Experimental implications: — Manipulating global coordination mechanisms (e.g., bioelectric signaling, mechanical coupling) should redirect morphogenesis even when local cellular machinery remains intact. Small, distributed perturbations to global constraints should produce larger-scale pattern changes than local perturbations alone. Test cases: — Bioelectric modulation experiments altering membrane potential patterns.

— Mechanical boundary manipulation in developing tissues. — Distributed signaling interference versus localized genetic knockouts.

## 13.2 Repair Dynamics Depend on Global Constraint Integrity

Prediction: Repair and regeneration will fail not primarily when local growth mechanisms are disrupted, but when global coherence constraints are degraded. Experimental implications: — Tissues with intact cellular proliferation but disrupted global coordination should regenerate incorrectly or not at all. — Restoration of global signals should rescue repair even if local damage persists. Test cases: — Selective disruption of long-range signaling during regeneration. — Restoration of global pattern cues following severe injury. — Comparative studies of organisms with differing regenerative capacities.

## 13.3 Novel problem solving correlates with coherence flexibility

Prediction: Organisms capable of navigating a broader range of coherence landscapes will exhibit greater capacity for novel problem solving within a lifetime. Experimental implications: — Systems with richer regulatory architectures should adapt more successfully to unprecedented perturbations. — Artificially constraining regulatory flexibility should reduce novelty even if basic survival mechanisms remain intact. Test cases: — Comparative studies across species with varying developmental plasticity. — Experimental restriction of regulatory degrees of freedom. — Longitudinal observation of adaptive responses to novel environments.

## 13.4 Evolution Stabilizes Coherence-Navigating Architectures

Prediction: Evolution will preferentially stabilize architectures that support real-time coherence navigation, not just specific trait values. Experimental implications: — Lineages exposed to variable or unpredictable environments should evolve greater regulatory flexibility rather than narrowly optimized traits. — Evolutionary innovations should cluster around new coherence scales (e.g., multicellularity, nervous systems). Test cases: — Experimental evolution under fluctuating versus stable conditions. — Comparative genomic and developmental analyses of robustness and plasticity. — Analysis of major evolutionary transitions as coherence reorganizations.

## 13.5 Identifying Operators of Coherence

Beyond qualitative predictions, the framework suggests a concrete methodological goal: identifying the operators that govern coherence dynamics. These include: — Local operators responsible for fast, component-level dynamics. — Global operators responsible for enforcing large-scale integration. Experimental strategy: — Perturb systems at different scales and measure recovery trajectories. — Identify variables whose disruption disproportionately affects global coherence. — Use dynamical modeling to infer operator structure from system responses. Such approaches move beyond correlation toward causal identification of coherence-maintaining mechanisms.

## 13.6 Falsifiability and Limits

The coherence framework is falsifiable. It would be undermined if: biological systems routinely fail to reorganize in response to perturbation despite intact global coordination, — adaptive novelty occurs in the absence of coherence-preserving dynamics, — or long-range constraints prove unnecessary for stability and repair. By specifying where and how the framework could fail, we invite empirical scrutiny rather than immunizing the theory against refutation.

## 13.7 Summary

Treating coherence as a central biological constraint generates a unified experimental agenda. It shifts attention from isolated mechanisms to integrative dynamics, from static structures to recovery trajectories, and from narrow optimization to persistent viability. The framework does not replace existing biological methods; it reorganizes them around a common explanatory axis. In doing so, it opens new pathways for investigating development, regeneration, adaptation, and evolution within a single coherent theoretical structure. We conclude by situating these claims within their broader implications and acknowledging the limits and scope of the present work.

This section has specified the framework's empirical commitments: threshold predictions for coherence collapse, scaling relationships across biological organization, and experimental designs that could falsify the central claims. The predictions are specific enough to be tested with current methods and general enough to apply across biological scales — from prebiotic chemistry to evolutionary dynamics.

# Section 14: Discussion, Limitations, and Conclusion

This paper has advanced a coherence-based framework for understanding biological organization across scales, from prebiotic chemistry through cellular regulation, organismal development, and evolutionary dynamics. By treating coherence as a dynamical constraint rather than a metaphor or mentalistic property, we have shown how diverse biological phenomena — the origin of life, regulation, repair, novel problem solving, and evolutionary convergence — can be understood within a unified explanatory structure. At its core, the framework reframes biology as the study of systems that must preserve integrated organization under continuous constraint. Living systems persist not because they are static or

optimized, but because they are capable of reorganizing in response to disruption. Coherence, in this sense, is not a property that systems possess once and for all; it is a condition that must be continually earned.

## 14.1 What This Framework Adds to Existing Biology

The coherence-based perspective does not replace established biological theories. Evolution by natural selection, molecular genetics, developmental biology, and systems biology remain indispensable. What this framework offers is a way of integrating these domains around a common explanatory axis. Rather than treating the origin of life, development, regeneration, and adaptation as separate problems, coherence dynamics reveal their shared structure. Rather than viewing evolution as a blind search, coherence constraints clarify why certain solutions recur and persist. Rather than invoking intelligence only at the level of nervous systems, the framework explains how intelligence-like behavior emerges naturally in embedded biological systems. In this way, coherence serves as a unifying constraint that connects mechanism to function without invoking cognition, representation, or design.

## 14.2 Limits of the Present Account

Several limitations must be acknowledged. First, coherence is not directly observable as a single variable; it must be inferred from system behavior, recovery trajectories, and integration across scales. Operationalizing coherence in specific experimental contexts remains an open challenge. Second, the mathematical framework presented here is intentionally minimal. While it establishes coherence as a dynamical property, further formal work will be required to specify coherence functionals for particular biological systems and to identify their associated operators empirically. Third, while the abiogenesis analysis (Section 4) addresses the transition from nonlife to life, the discursive middle sections (V—IX) focus primarily on biological systems that exhibit strong regulatory and regenerative capacities. How coherence dynamics operate in simpler organisms, minimal life forms, and artificial protocells warrants further empirical investigation.

## 14.3 Abiogenesis and the Completeness of the Biological Account

The abiogenesis analysis (Section 4) completes the framework's engagement with the three central open questions in biology. The coherence framework now offers a continuous account spanning from prebiotic chemistry through the origin of life, individual development, and evolutionary dynamics. No additional principles are required to transition from one domain to the next.

This reframing has consequences beyond mere completeness. It grounds the coherence framework in biology's deepest question, demonstrating that coherence dynamics can generate novel insight — not merely redescribe known biology in new vocabulary. It connects the mathematical framework of Section 2 directly to origin-of-life research through testable predictions (§4.5). And it reveals the structural unity among biology's three mysteries: the same dynamical requirement — maintenance of viability within constrained regions of state space — operates at the chemical scale (abiogenesis), the organismal scale (morphogenesis), and the population scale (evolution).

## 14.4 Biological Identity as Constraint Continuity

The expanded treatment of biological identity (§2.8) introduces a perspective that cuts across several sections of this paper. By defining identity as the continuity of a constraint manifold rather than the persistence of material substrate, the framework provides precise answers to questions that purely compositional or informational accounts leave unresolved.

The organism-as-standing-process view connects naturally to the thermodynamic analysis of Section 3 (coherence requires continuous energy throughput), the multi-scale analysis of Section 6 (identity is maintained across nested levels of organization), and the evolutionary analysis of Section 10 (evolution selects for systems that maintain constraint continuity under perturbation). It also provides the conceptual foundation for the coherence ladder (Appendix C), where the transition from physical to biological coherence corresponds precisely to the transition from passive persistence to constraint-preserved identity.

The implications extend beyond the biological domain. The constraint-continuity account of identity provides the structural basis for psychological identity (developed in the Psychology companion paper) and for the analysis of artificial system persistence (developed in the AI companion paper). In each case, the same formal apparatus — constraint manifolds, deformation metrics, attractor dynamics — applies, though the specific constraints and the mechanisms of their maintenance differ across domains.

**14.5 Scope discipline and future directions**

The framework developed here

is biological in scope. While it has implications for cognition, artificial systems, and social organization, those extensions require careful treatment and empirical grounding. This paper has deliberately avoided importing claims about consciousness, meaning, or ethics into the biological analysis. Future work may explore how coherence dynamics scale into cognitive systems, how artificial systems differ in their relationship to coherence costs, and how coherence constraints shape institutional or ecological stability. These extensions should build on biological foundations rather than bypass them.

## 14.6 Conclusion: What Biology Teaches Us about Persistence

Biology reveals that persistence is neither automatic nor guaranteed. Living systems exist in a narrow corridor between order and collapse, sustained by continuous regulation, repair, and reorganization. Coherence is the condition that makes this persistence possible, and its maintenance defines the work of life. By treating coherence as a central biological constraint, we gain a clearer understanding of how life first arose from nonliving matter, how organisms develop and adapt, and how evolution produces complexity — how living systems solve problems they have never encountered before, and why certain forms recur across the history of life. Biology, in this view, does not merely catalog living things; it exposes the limits within which life can endure. Biology shows us not what must exist, but what cannot persist.

# References

Baluška, F., & Levin, M. (2016). On having no head: Cognition throughout biological systems. *Frontiers in Psychology*, 7, 902.

Bich, L., & Moreno, A. (2016). The role of regulation in the origin and synthetic modelling of minimal cognition. *Biosystems*, 148, 12–21.

Deacon, T. W. (2012). *Incomplete Nature: How Mind Emerged from Matter*. W. W. Norton.

England, J. L. (2013). Statistical physics of self-replication. *Journal of Chemical Physics*, 139(12), 121923.

England, J. L. (2015). Dissipative adaptation in driven self-assembly. *Nature Nanotechnology*, 10, 919–923.

Fields, C., & Levin, M. (2022). Competency in navigating arbitrary spaces as an invariant for analyzing cognition in diverse embodiments. *Entropy*, 24(6), 819.

Friston, K. (2010). The free-energy principle: A unified brain theory? *Nature Reviews Neuroscience*, 11(2), 127–138.

Friston, K. (2013). Life as we know it. *Journal of the Royal Society Interface*, 10(86), 20130475.

Gilbert, S. F., & Epel, D. (2009). *Ecological Developmental Biology: Integrating Epigenetics, Medicine, and Evolution*. Sinauer Associates.

Goodwin, B. (1994). *How the Leopard Changed Its Spots: The Evolution of Complexity*. Scribner.

Hordijk, W., & Steel, M. (2004). Detecting autocatalytic, self-sustaining sets in chemical reaction systems. *Journal of Theoretical Biology*, 227(4), 451–461.

Jaeger, J., & Monk, N. (2014). Bioattractors: Dynamical systems theory and the evolution of regulatory processes. *Journal of Physiology*, 592(11), 2267–2281.

Kauffman, S. A. (1993). *The Origins of Order: Self-Organization and Selection in Evolution*. Oxford University Press.

Kauffman, S. A. (2000). *Investigations*. Oxford University Press.

Kirschner, M., & Gerhart, J. (2005). *The Plausibility of Life: Resolving Darwin's Dilemma*. Yale University Press.

Kriegman, S., Blackiston, D., Levin, M., & Bongard, J. (2020). A scalable pipeline for designing reconfigurable organisms. *Proceedings of the National Academy of Sciences*, 117(4), 1853–1859.

Lane, N. (2015). *The Vital Question: Energy, Evolution, and the Origins of Complex Life*. W. W. Norton.

Levin, M. (2014). Molecular bioelectricity: What do protons know about cognition? *BioEssays*, 36(10), 957–967.

Levin, M. (2021). Bioelectric signaling: Reprogrammable circuits underlying embryogenesis, regeneration, and cancer. *Cell*, 184(6), 1971–1989.

Levin, M., & Dennett, D. C. (2020). Cognition all the way down. *Aeon*.

Lyon, P. (2006). The biogenic approach to cognition. *Cognitive Processing*, 7(1), 11–29.

Martin, W., & Russell, M. J. (2007). On the origin of biochemistry at an alkaline hydrothermal vent. *Philosophical Transactions of the Royal Society B*, 362(1486), 1887–1925.

Maturana, H. R., & Varela, F. J. (1980). *Autopoiesis and Cognition: The Realization of the Living*. D. Reidel Publishing.

Moreno, A., & Mossio, M. (2015). *Biological Autonomy: A Philosophical and Theoretical Enquiry*. Springer.

Moreno, A., & Ruiz-Mirazo, K. (2009). The problem of the emergence of functional diversity in prebiotic evolution. *Biology & Philosophy*, 24(5), 585–605.

Newman, S. A., & Müller, G. B. (2000). Epigenetic mechanisms of character origination. *Journal of Experimental Zoology*, 288(4), 304–317.

Nicolis, G., & Prigogine, I. (1977). *Self-Organization in Non-equilibrium Systems*. Wiley-Interscience.

Noble, D. (2006). *The Music of Life: Biology Beyond the Genome*. Oxford University Press.

Prigogine, I., & Stengers, I. (1984). *Order Out of Chaos: Man's New Dialogue with Nature*. Bantam Books.

Ruiz-Mirazo, K., Briones, C., & de la Escosura, A. (2014). Prebiotic systems chemistry: New perspectives for the origins of life. *Chemical Reviews*, 114(1), 285–366.

Schreiber, T. (2000). Measuring information transfer. *Physical Review Letters*, 85(2), 461–464.

Schrödinger, E. (1944). *What Is Life?* Cambridge University Press.

Szostak, J. W., Bartel, D. P., & Luisi, P. L. (2001). Synthesizing life. *Nature*, 409(6818), 387–390.

Thompson, E. (2007). *Mind in Life: Biology, Phenomenology, and the Sciences of Mind.* Harvard University Press.

Tononi, G. (2004). An information integration theory of consciousness. *BMC Neuroscience*, 5, 42.

Varela, F. J., Maturana, H. R., & Uribe, R. (1974). Autopoiesis: The organization of living systems, its characterization and a model. *Biosystems*, 5(4), 187–196.

Wächtershäuser, G. (1988). Before enzymes and templates: Theory of surface metabolism. *Microbiological Reviews*, 52(4), 452–484.

Waddington, C. H. (1957). *The Strategy of the Genes.* George Allen & Unwin.

Wagner, A. (2014). *Arrival of the Fittest: Solving Evolution's Greatest Puzzle.* Current.

Walker, S. I., & Davies, P. C. W. (2013). The algorithmic origins of life. *Journal of the Royal Society Interface*, 10(79), 20120869.

Walsh, D. M. (2015). *Organisms, Agency, and Evolution.* Cambridge University Press.

West-Eberhard, M. J. (2003). *Developmental Plasticity and Evolution.* Oxford University Press.

Rader, G. K. D. (2026a). Coherence Universalism — Metaphysics and Epistemology: Coherence Logic and an Introduction to the Coherence Ladder. Heaven≡Earth Press.

Rader, G. K. D. (2026b). Coherence Universalism — Foundations: The Principle Architecture. Heaven≡Earth Press.

Rader, G. K. D. (2026c). Coherence Universalism — Physics: Coherence Dynamics, Emergent Spacetime, and the Laws of Physical Order. Heaven≡Earth Press.

Rader, G. K. D. (2026d). Coherence Universalism — Biology: Coherence as the Organizing Principle of Living Systems. Heaven≡Earth Press.

Rader, G. K. D. (2026e). Coherence Universalism — Psychology: Coherence as the Structural Foundation of Mind, Meaning, and Mental Health. Heaven≡Earth Press.

Rader, G. K. D. (2026f). Coherence Universalism — Consciousness: Why Experience Is Constituted by Coherence Under Constraint. Heaven≡Earth Press.

Rader, G. K. D. (2026g). Coherence Universalism — Ethics: Values, Normative Orientation, and Justificatory Integrity. Heaven≡Earth Press.

Rader, G. K. D. (2026h). Coherence Universalism — Social Dynamics: Coherence Strategies, Institutional Design, and the Present Crisis. Heaven≡Earth Press.

Rader, G. K. D. (2026i). Coherence Universalism — Artificial Intelligence: Consciousness, Alignment, and the Future of Intelligence. Heaven≡Earth Press.

# Appendix A: Formalization of Coherence-Constrained Dynamics

This appendix provides a more explicit formal account of the coherencebased framework used throughout the paper. It is intended to clarify the mathematical assumptions underlying the main text, not to introduce new claims or require advanced formal background. All results discussed here are consistent with, and subordinate to, the biological arguments developed in the main body.

**A.1 System State Space**

We represent a biological system at time t by a state vector: $x(t) = (x_1, x_2, \ldots , x_n)$

where each component $x_i$ corresponds to a biologically relevant variable at the scale of interest (e.g., molecular concentrations, membrane potentials, tissue configurations, physiological states). The dimensionality and interpretation of x depend on context. The framework does not assume a privileged level of description. System dynamics are given by: $dx/dt = F(x, e, t)$ where: — F captures intrinsic system dynamics, — e represents environmental inputs and constraints, — t denotes time.

**A.2 The Coherence Functional**

We define a scalar coherence functional: $C(x) \geq 0$ interpreted as a measure of integrated biological viability. Properties of C(x): — C(x) is high for states that support coordinated function and persistence. C(x) decreases as integration degrades. — $C(x) = 0$ corresponds to irreversible loss of biological identity (e.g., death). C(x) is not equivalent to entropy, order, efficiency, or fitness alone. A state may be ordered yet biologically incoherent, or efficient yet globally unstable. Coherence reflects functional integration across scales.

**A.3 Coherence Gradients and Directionality**

The coherence functional

induces a gradient over state space: $\nabla C(x)$ This gradient defines directions of increasing or decreasing coherence. Biological systems subject to perturbation tend to evolve toward regions of higher coherence, not because they compute this gradient explicitly, but because incoherent states are dynamically unstable. Directionality in biological behavior thus arises from constraint, not intention. Coherence gradients bias system trajectories without requiring foresight, representation, or optimization.

A.4 Local and Global Operators

To capture multi-scale biological

organization, we distinguish between two classes of operators: — Local operators, D(x), governing fast, component-level dynamics (e.g., enzymatic reactions, ion channel behavior, local signaling). — Global operators, G(x), enforcing slower, integrative constraints (e.g., tissue patterning, organism-wide bioelectric fields, developmental targets). System dynamics can be written schematically as: $dx/dt = D(x) + G(x) + E(x, t)$ where $E(x, t)$ represents external perturbations. A central claim of the framework is that biological coherence depends on the interaction between D and G. Local dynamics alone cannot account for stable form, repair, or regeneration.

**A.5 Attractors, Basins, and Viability Regions**

of state space

corresponding to stable biological organization form viable basins. Within these basins, trajectories converge toward attractors representing coherent biological states. Biological attractors differ from simple physical attractors in that they are: — deformable under environmental pressure, — history-dependent, — capable of reorganization following perturbation. Development, regeneration, and adaptation can be interpreted as trajectories that seek re-entry into viable basins after displacement.

**A.6 Irreversibility and Coherence Collapse**

Not all departures from

coherence are recoverable. If perturbations push the system beyond critical thresholds, recovery dynamics may no longer exist. This corresponds to irreversible coherence collapse. Such thresholds explain why biological failure is often abrupt rather than gradual, and why energy availability alone is insufficient to restore life once global integration is lost.

**A.7 Memory and Path Dependence**

Biological systems exhibit memory: past

states influence future dynamics. This can be represented by allowing coherence to depend on system history: C(x, H) where H summarizes accumulated structural, regulatory, or epigenetic modifications. This formulation captures learning, developmental canalization, immune memory, and evolutionary inheritance without invoking symbolic storage.

**A.8 Coherence versus Optimization**

Finally, it is important to

distinguish coherence from optimization. Optimization seeks maximal values of specific variables. Coherence seeks sustained integration under constraint. Locally

optimized states may reduce global coherence, increasing fragility. Biological persistence therefore prioritizes repair, robustness, and reintegration over maximal performance.

A.9 Summary

This appendix formalizes the minimal mathematical

commitments of the coherence-based framework: — Biological systems occupy structured state spaces. — Coherence can be represented as a scalar functional. — Directionality arises from coherence gradients. Multi-scale operators enforce integration. — Viability depends on remaining within coherence-supporting basins. These formal elements support, but do not replace, the empirical arguments presented in the main text.

# Appendix B: Mapping the Biology Paper to the Foundations of Coherence

Universalism This appendix situates the present biology paper within the broader framework of Coherence Universalism (CU) as articulated in Foundations of Coherence Universalism (v0.09) Foundations Doc (Claude Edit) . The main body of this paper has been written to stand alone as a contribution to theoretical biology. No prior familiarity with CU is required to understand its arguments. This appendix is provided for readers who wish to see how the biological claims developed here relate to the larger system of foundational principles, dynamics, and diagnostics that comprise Coherence Universalism. The mapping below is interpretive rather than prescriptive. It does not claim that the biology paper "derives from" the Foundations document. Rather, it shows how the biological results instantiate, support, and constrain specific CU principles.

**B.1 Status of the Biology Paper**

Within CU Within Coherence Universalism,

the biology paper plays a grounding role. — It is not an application of CU to biology. — It is one of the empirical anchors that justifies CU's broader claims about coherence, normativity, and constraint. Biological coherence provides the first domain in which coherence becomes active, selfmaintaining, and problem-solving under real-world constraint. For this reason, several biology-specific principles (CU-B1 through CU-B4) have been added to the Foundations document after the initial compilation of the spine. These principles are empirically motivated and should be read as mid-level constraints, not metaphysical axioms.

**B.2 Mapping to Foundational Principles (CU-FP)**

The biology paper

directly supports and operationalizes the following foundational principles: — CU-FP1 (Coherence as a Transcendental Condition) Biology demonstrates that persistence, function, and identity in living systems are impossible without coherence. Life makes the transcendental claim empirically unavoidable. — CU-FP2 (Coherence Admits of Degree and Direction) Development, regeneration, and adaptation are inherently graded and directional processes. Organisms demonstrably move through coherence landscapes rather than occupying static states.

— CU-FP3 (Constraint Is Essential to Coherence) Biological regulation only functions because organisms are constrained by energetic limits, environmental resistance, and irreversibility. Coherence without constraint does not occur in living systems. — CU-FP4 (Multi-Scale Coherence) The failure of local mechanisms to explain global patterning, regeneration, and robustness directly motivates a multi-scale coherence account. — CU-FP5 (Non-Reduction) Biological coherence is real without being fundamental substance. Molecular explanations remain valid but incomplete without integrative constraints. — CU-FP7 (Coherence Collapse) Biological failure modes — burnout, developmental arrest, pathological regeneration, organismal death — exemplify collapse through fragmentation rather than simple destruction.

**B.3 Mapping to Dynamical Principles (CU-D)**

The biology paper is the

clearest empirical instantiation of CU's dynamical backbone: — CU-D1 (Universal Flow / Update Rule) Biological regulation, learning, and repair are concrete examples of coherence-guided update under constraint. — CU-D2 (Coherence Drive) Apparent purposiveness in organisms is explained without teleology as selection pressure toward coherence preservation. — CU-D4 (Coherence Gradients) Developmental trajectories, regenerative target morphology, and adaptive novelty follow gradients rather than explicit optimization. — CU-D5 (Non-Equilibrium Stability)

Living systems persist far from equilibrium and require continuous maintenance. Static stability corresponds to loss of life. — CU-D9 (Multi-Scale Failure Modes) Biological pathologies routinely arise from scale mismatches rather than local defects, providing canonical examples of CU-D9 dynamics.

B.4 Biology-Specific Principles Added to the Foundations (CU-B)

The following principles were refined during the drafting of this paper and have been incorporated into the Foundations document as CU-B1 through CU-B4: — CU-B1 — Biological Coherence as Active Self-Maintenance Living systems are distinguished by active preservation of integrated organization under constraint. — CU-B2 — Coherence-Driven Novel Problem Solving Organisms can solve problems with no evolutionary precedent by navigating coherence gradients rather than executing fixed programs. — CU-B3 — Global Constraint Precedes Local Optimization Developmental and regenerative outcomes are governed by global integrative constraints, not by aggregation of local optima. CU-B4 — Evolution Stabilizes Coherence-Navigating Architectures Evolution preferentially preserves regulatory architectures capable of maintaining coherence across perturbations, not merely specific traits. These principles are empirically grounded and should be read as constraints on biological explanation, not speculative metaphysics.

**B.5 Relation to Later CU Domains**

The biology paper establishes

conditions that later CU domains presuppose: — Epistemology: Biological constraint sensitivity and regulation ground EL-0 through EL-2. Consciousness: Biological coherence is necessary but not sufficient for consciousness; it defines the pre-valence regime. — Ethics and Politics: Multi-scale coherence in organisms foreshadows the Local—Global Coherence Principle. — Artificial Intelligence: The contrast between intrinsic biological coherence and externally scaffolded artificial coherence underwrites CU's AI safety claims. In this sense, biology is not one domain among many. It is the pivot between physics and normativity.

**B.6 Summary**

This appendix clarifies how the biology paper fits within the overall structure of Coherence Universalism: — The paper stands alone scientifically. — It grounds key CU principles empirically. — It motivates later extensions without presupposing them. — It constrains speculative claims by anchoring them in biological reality. Readers interested only in biological theory may safely ignore this appendix. Readers interested in CU as a unified framework should treat the biology paper as one of its primary empirical foundations.

# Appendix C: The Coherence Ladder (Biological Context)

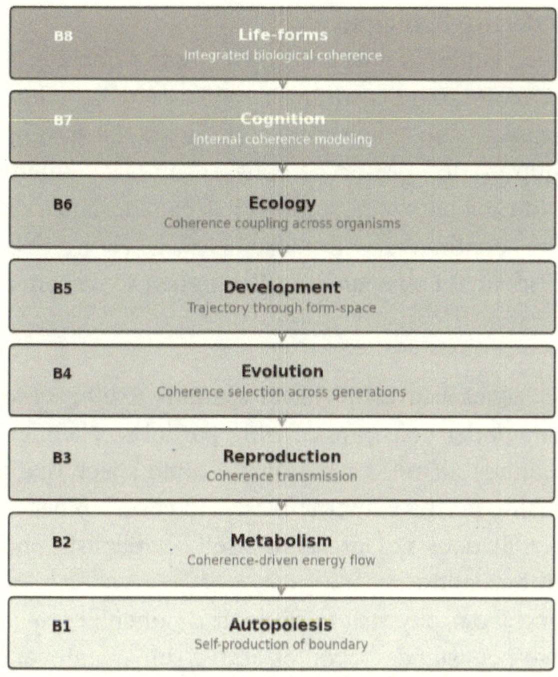


*Figure 8. The Coherence Ladder in biological context. Biology*

occupies the central rungs between physical coherence (passive persistence) and psychological coherence (representation-dependent). The abiogenesis threshold marks the transition from passive to active coherence maintenance. The four biological rungs — metabolic coherence, self-maintenance, adaptive constraint satisfaction, and life — are the focus of the present paper.

This appendix introduces the Coherence Ladder as a conceptual framework for understanding how different domains of structure, regulation, and agency arise as coherence stabilizes under increasing constraint. The ladder is not an evolutionary timeline, nor a hierarchy of value. It is a statement of explanatory dependence: certain forms of organization cannot arise unless more basic coherence conditions are already in place. The main body of this paper focuses on biological coherence. The ladder is included here to clarify how biological phenomena fit within a broader coherence-based ordering, and to situate biological selfmaintenance between physical structure and psychological agency.

### C.1 The Ordering Principle

The coherence ladder is governed by a single principle: As coherence stabilizes under increasing constraint, new forms of structure and regulation become unavoidable. Each rung introduces the minimal additional constraint required to preserve coherence at a higher level of organization. No rung adds a new metaphysical substance or explanatory primitive. Each is continuous with those below it, yet irreducible to them.

### C.2 From Physical Coherence to Biological Coherence:

The Abiogenesis

Threshold

At the most general level, physical systems exhibit coherence when structure persists under constraint. Stable particles, chemical bonds, and dissipative structures all reflect regions of state space that are easier to occupy and maintain than alternatives. However, physical coherence alone is passive. It does not preserve itself. It persists only so long as boundary conditions allow.

The transition from physical to biological coherence — the threshold at which passive persistence becomes active self-maintenance — is precisely the abiogenesis transition analyzed in Section 4. This transition marks the first appearance of a new dynamical regime on the coherence ladder: a regime in which the system's continued coherence becomes a governing constraint on its own dynamics.

The abiogenesis threshold can be located precisely within the coherence ladder by the recurrence criterion developed in §4.1:

$$P(s_{t+1} \in L \mid s_t \in L) > P(s_{t+1} \in L \mid s_t \notin L)$$

Below this threshold, structure persists passively. Above it, structure causes its own persistence. The transition is sharp in dynamical character — the system's qualitative behavior changes at the threshold — even though the underlying physical variables change continuously.

The ladder below the biological threshold includes several sub-rungs that represent progressive approaches to the transition without crossing it:

Equilibrium structure (crystals, stable molecules, geological formations): Coherence is maintained by energetic favorability. No energy throughput required. No active maintenance. Perturbation leads to degradation, not repair.

Far-from-equilibrium structure (convection cells, vortices, chemical oscillations): Coherence requires energy throughput and is maintained by dissipation. These structures are prolonged but not self-constraining — they persist only as long as external driving continues in the right form.

Pre-living chemical complexity (autocatalytic reactions, compartmentalized chemistry, catalytic surfaces): Coherence begins to exhibit self-reinforcing dynamics but has not yet crossed the recurrence threshold. The system produces conditions partially favorable to its own continuation but cannot reliably regenerate after perturbation.

Proto-life: the system crosses the recurrence threshold. Environmental dynamics, as modified by the structure's own activity, regenerate the structure after disruption. Destruction triggers reconstruction. At this point, the system has become a preferred future state of the environment it modifies. This is the abiogenesis threshold — the first rung of biological coherence.

The subsequent biological rungs of the ladder — metabolic coherence, self-maintenance, adaptive constraint satisfaction, life — build on this foundation by elaborating increasingly sophisticated mechanisms for maintaining and extending the constraint structure established at the abiogenesis threshold. Each rung adds new regulatory capacity without introducing new ontological primitives. The transition from physics to biology is continuous in principle but sharp in dynamical character: it is the moment at which coherence begins to cause itself.

## C.3 The Biological Rungs of the Coherence Ladder

Within the ladder framework, biological systems occupy a distinct regime characterized by active coherence preservation. The following rungs are most relevant to the present paper.

### *C.3.1 Far-From-Equilibrium Structure*

Biological systems operate far from thermodynamic equilibrium. Unlike equilibrium structures, they require continuous throughput of energy and matter to persist. This establishes the physical precondition for life but does not yet constitute life itself. At this stage, coherence is prolonged, but not yet self-constraining.

### *C.3.2 Metabolic Coherence*

Metabolic coherence arises when internal processes actively reorganize energy and matter to stabilize structure. The system no longer merely benefits from favorable flows; it regulates them. Metabolism introduces directed internal dynamics, but these dynamics still operate without reference to long-term identity or continuity.

### *C.3.3 Self-Maintenance*

Self-maintenance marks a qualitative transition. The system's continued coherence becomes a governing constraint on its own dynamics. Processes that undermine coherence are suppressed; processes that restore it are favored. At this rung: — Coherence is no longer an outcome but a requirement. — Failure modes correspond to loss of identity rather than mere inefficiency. — Repair and regulation become intrinsic rather than incidental. This transition distinguishes living systems from merely complex physical ones.

### *C.3.4 Adaptive Constraint Satisfaction*

Adaptive constraint satisfaction arises when a self-maintaining system can modify how it preserves coherence in response to novel conditions. This capacity explains: — Robust development under perturbation Regeneration after injury — Problem-solving in environments with no evolutionary precedent adaptation here does not require representation, planning, or cognition. It emerges from the system's ability to reorganize constraints in response to coherence gradients.

### *C.3.5 Life*

Within the coherence ladder, life is defined functionally: Life is coherence that actively resists its own dissipation through self-maintenance and adaptive constraint satisfaction. This definition does not depend on particular molecular substrates, evolutionary histories, or taxonomic categories. It unifies biological diversity under a single organizational criterion.

## C.4 Relation to Evolution

The coherence ladder is not an alternative to evolutionary theory. Rather, it clarifies what evolution selects for. Evolution stabilizes architectures that: — maintain coherence under perturbation, — navigate coherence gradients effectively, — and preserve viability across changing conditions. From this perspective, natural selection does not create coherence ex nihilo. It discovers and amplifies regulatory structures that already satisfy coherence constraints. This explains why: — certain forms recur across evolutionary history, — developmental pathways are canalized, — and organisms solve novel problems without direct evolutionary precedent.

### C.5 Boundary to Higher Rungs

The present paper stops at biological coherence. Higher rungs of the ladder introduce additional constraints not required for biological explanation, including: — Internal models and predictive coherence (psychology) — Shared representations and coordination (social systems) — Norm justification and value tradeoffs (ethics) — Engineered optimization and alignment (artificial systems) These domains presuppose biological coherence but are not reducible to it. They are treated in separate papers within the Coherence Universalism program.

### C.6 Why the Ladder Matters for Biology

The coherence ladder serves three functions in the biological context: 1. Clarification It distinguishes biological self-maintenance from both physical stability and psychological agency. 2. Unification It shows how development, regeneration, adaptation, and evolution share a common coherence logic. 3. Discipline It prevents biological explanation from drifting prematurely into cognition, teleology, or normativity. By locating biology precisely on the ladder, we preserve its explanatory power while recognizing its continuity with broader coherence dynamics.

### C.7 Summary

This appendix has shown how biological systems occupy a specific and indispensable region of the coherence ladder: — Above passive physical structure

— Below representational and normative systems — Defined by active, adaptive coherence preservation Understanding biology through this lens clarifies why living systems are robust, flexible, and capable of solving problems their evolutionary history did not explicitly encode. The coherence ladder thus provides an ordering principle that unifies biological explanation without expanding its scope beyond what the evidence requires.

# Appendix D: Relation to Existing Biological and Theoretical Frameworks

This appendix situates the coherence-based framework developed in this paper within the landscape of existing biological and theoretical approaches. The goal is not to claim novelty through opposition, but to clarify how coherence dynamics integrate, extend, and reinterpret established lines of research. This appendix is intentionally non--exhaustive. It highlights frameworks that bear directly on the core claims of the paper.

**D.1 Systems Biology and Network Regulation**

Key overlap — Emphasis on

interactions over components — Network-level dynamics — Robustness, redundancy, and degeneracy — Nonlinear feedback and emergent behavior Distinction — Systems biology often catalogs interactions without specifying why certain global organizations persist. — The coherence framework introduces viability as a constraint, explaining why some network configurations are stable while others are transient or pathological. Contribution — Coherence provides a unifying criterion for evaluating system-level organization beyond descriptive network structure.

**D.2 Evo-Devo and Developmental Bias**

Key overlap — Development constrains

evolutionary trajectories — Phenotypic variation is structured, not uniform — Canalization and reuse of developmental pathways Distinction Evo-devo identifies constraints but often treats them as historical or mechanistic facts.

— The coherence framework explains these constraints as consequences of maintaining integrated organization across scales. Contribution Evolutionary outcomes are interpreted as flow through coherence-constrained developmental landscapes, rather than as accumulation of isolated trait optimizations.

**D.3 Morphogenetic Fields and Pattern Formation**

Key overlap — Global

pattern regulation — Robustness of form — Long-range coordination during development and regeneration Distinction — Classical morphogenetic field concepts often remain qualitative. — The coherence framework formalizes field-like behavior as global operators shaping system dynamics in state space. Contribution — Provides a dynamical interpretation of morphogenetic fields grounded in coherence maintenance.

**D.4 Bioelectricity and Long-Range Signaling**

Key overlap — Non-neural

electrical signaling — Control of large-scale patterning — Modulation of developmental and regenerative outcomes Distinction — Bioelectric studies demonstrate that long-range control exists. — The coherence framework explains why such control is necessary: local regulation alone cannot preserve organism-level coherence. Contribution — Positions bioelectricity as a key mechanism of global coherence enforcement rather than a special-purpose signaling system.

**D.5 Homeostasis, Allostasis, and Predictive Regulation**

Key overlap

Regulation in response to perturbation — Anticipatory and adaptive control — Maintenance of internal stability under change

Distinction — Homeostasis and allostasis describe how regulation occurs. — Coherence explains what regulation is ultimately for: preserving integrated viability rather than fixed variables. Contribution — Unifies regulatory concepts under a single coherence-maintenance imperative.

**D.6 Robustness, Resilience, and Degeneracy**

Key overlap — Functional

persistence under perturbation — Multiple pathways to similar outcomes Fault tolerance in biological systems Distinction — Robustness is often treated as a property to be explained. — The coherence framework treats robustness as a necessary consequence of operating near viability thresholds. Contribution — Explains why biological systems are robust by necessity, not by optimization.

**D.7 Constraint-Based Explanation in Biology**

Key overlap — Increasing

emphasis on constraints rather than causes alone — Recognition that not all explanations are mechanistic — Interest in boundary conditions and feasibility spaces Distinction — Constraint-based explanations are often invoked locally. — Coherence provides a global organizing constraint that integrates multiple constraint types (energetic, developmental, organizational). Contribution — Positions coherence as a unifying constraint that operates across levels and timescales.

**D.8 What This Framework Does Not Claim**

To avoid misinterpretation, it is

important to emphasize that the coherence framework: — Does not invoke teleology or design — Does not deny evolutionary theory — Does not require cognition, representation, or consciousness

— Does not replace mechanistic explanation Instead, it complements existing approaches by clarifying the conditions under which mechanisms can succeed.

**D.9 Summary: Integration Without Reduction**

The coherence-based framework

does not compete with established biological theories. It integrates them by identifying a shared constraint: the need to maintain integrated organization under continuous disruption. By situating development, regeneration, adaptation, and evolution within coherence-constrained dynamics, the framework provides a common explanatory backbone while preserving the empirical insights of diverse biological traditions.

Appendix E: Evolution, Constraint, and a Coherence-Based Vision of Science

Evolution by natural selection is among the most successful explanatory frameworks in the history of science. It accounts for adaptation, diversity, and complexity without invoking foresight or design, and it is supported by an overwhelming body of empirical evidence. Any theory that seeks to reinterpret biological organization must therefore clarify its relationship to evolutionary explanation. This appendix does three things. First, it situates the coherence-based framework developed in this paper within mainstream evolutionary biology. Second, it clarifies the role of constraint as a legitimate and necessary form of scientific explanation. Finally, it articulates a broader vision of science that follows naturally from the empirical results discussed here—a vision that is grounded in fact, yet no longer bound to unsupported metaphysical assumptions about randomness, meaninglessness, or indifference in the universe.

**E.1 Evolution as a foundational scientific achievement**

Darwin's central

insight was that complex, functional biological organization can arise through variation and selection without foresight or intention. This insight remains one of the great intellectual achievements of modern science. Evolutionary theory explains how traits are filtered across generations and why organisms appear well adapted to their environments. Nothing in the coherence-based framework developed in this paper challenges this core account. Variation remains stochastic with respect to fitness. Selection remains differential survival and reproduction. Lineages change over time through inheritance, mutation, and drift. However, evolutionary theory has always left certain questions implicit rather than answered. In particular, it does not fully explain why viable biological organization occupies such a narrow, structured region of possibility space, nor why adaptive solutions cluster so strongly around recurring forms and architectures.

**E.2 Constraint as a mode of scientific explanation**

Across the sciences,

explanation increasingly involves identifying constraints rather than enumerating causal chains alone. In physics, conservation laws restrict what can occur regardless of initial conditions. In chemistry, bonding rules limit molecular configurations long before

reactions are considered. In engineering, material limits define feasible designs independently of intention. Biology is no exception. Developmental pathways, energetic requirements, physical laws, and regulatory architectures constrain which variations can persist long before natural selection acts. These constraints do not compete with causal explanations; they make them intelligible. The coherence-based framework identifies integrated viability as a central biological constraint. Living systems must maintain coherence under continuous perturbation. This requirement shapes the space of possible biological forms independently of historical contingency.

E.3 Directionality without teleology

Constraint-based explanations are

often mistaken for teleological ones. This confusion arises when directionality is equated with purpose. The coherence framework introduces directionality without intention. Systems move toward states that preserve coherence because incoherent states fail to persist. This is no more teleological than a river flowing downhill or a crystal forming under appropriate conditions. Evolutionary theory already relies on this kind of directionality. Selection favors persistence, not purpose. What coherence adds is an account of why persistence itself is structured—why some forms are reachable and others are not.

**E.4 Evolutionary novelty and coherence landscapes**

One of the enduring

puzzles in evolutionary biology concerns the origin of novelty. Mutation supplies variation, but the emergence of new functional organization often appears structured rather than arbitrary. Developmental bias, convergent evolution, and rapid adaptive reorganization all point toward non-random patterning. Within a coherence framework, this patterning is expected. Biological systems explore variation within structured coherence landscapes defined by the requirement to remain integrated. Novelty arises not from blind search alone, but from reorganization within constrained spaces of viability. Evolution stabilizes successful solutions across generations, but those solutions are often constructed dynamically by organisms navigating coherence constraints within their lifetimes. Evolution filters; coherence shapes.

**E.5 What coherence adds to evolutionary explanation**

The coherence-based

framework does not replace evolutionary theory. It clarifies what evolutionary processes are operating on. Selection does not act on arbitrary forms; it acts on systems already constrained by coherence requirements. Gene regulatory networks, developmental architectures, and physiological systems are not random encodings. They are structured responses to the problem of maintaining integration under real-world conditions. In this sense, evolution is not blind in the strongest metaphysical sense often implied. While it lacks foresight or intention, it unfolds within a universe whose structure already encodes coherence gradients. Randomness supplies exploration; coherence determines what can persist. Nothing in this account implies that future artificial systems could not generate coherence under genuine constraint; it implies only that current systems do not.

**E.6 From biological constraint to scientific worldview**

At this point, a

broader implication becomes unavoidable. The empirical results discussed in this paper show that life is not an improbable accident assembled against an indifferent backdrop. Rather, life is an expression of the fact that the universe admits stable, self-maintaining organization under constraint. Biological coherence is not imposed on the universe; it is made possible by the universe's structure. This claim does not invoke design, purpose, or external direction. It does not deny chance or contingency. It simply rejects the unsupported assumption that randomness is fundamental and order is merely local and accidental. What biology reveals instead is a universe in which coherence is real, costly, and consequential.

**E.7 A coherence-based vision of science**

The coherence framework points

toward a vision of science that is both rigorous and expansive. In this vision: — Randomness is real but not sovereign. — Constraint is as fundamental as causation. — Directionality does not require intention. Order does not require denial of chance. — Meaning is not imposed on the universe, but emerges wherever coherence stabilizes. This is not a return to pre-scientific teleology, nor a rejection of evolutionary explanation. It is an acknowledgment that the success of science has outgrown the metaphysical minimalism that once protected it from misuse. Biology, understood through coherence, shows that the universe is not indifferent to structure. It is structured in such a way that coherence can arise, persist, and complexify.

**E.8 Closing perspective**

The coherence-based framework developed in this

paper remains firmly grounded in empirical biology. Its claims are testable, falsifiable, and continuous with existing theory. Yet its implications extend beyond biology alone. By identifying coherence as a central constraint on living systems, we gain a clearer understanding of development, regeneration, adaptation, and evolution. We also gain a more intelligible picture of the universe itself—not as a meaningless backdrop occasionally punctuated by order, but as a domain in which order, under the right conditions, is possible and persistent. This is not a departure from science. It is a maturation of it.

# Appendix F: Glossary of Biology-Specific Terms

This glossary defines terms as used within the Coherence Universalism biology paper. For the full CU terminology, see the Master Glossary (Rader, 2026a).

**Adequacy (A(x)).** The aggregate constraint satisfaction of a biological system, measured as the geometric mean of individual viability constraint satisfactions. If any single constraint falls to zero, adequacy falls to zero regardless of other satisfactions.

**Attractor (coherence).** A region of state space where C(x) exceeds a viability minimum, trajectories remain stable under perturbation, and the coherence gradient $\nabla C$ points inward. Biological forms — cell types, body plans, developmental stages — correspond to coherence attractors.

**Basin of repair.** The maximum perturbation magnitude from which a system can recover and return to its coherence attractor. Measures biological resilience.

**Coherence collapse.** The loss of integrated biological organization, occurring when the system crosses below a critical threshold and cascade dynamics drive rapid disintegration. Types include fragmentation, exhaustion, catastrophic, and transformation.

**Coherence drive (CU-D3).** The persistent bias of living systems toward coherence-restoring dynamics, arising not from representation or foresight but from the filtering of non-viable configurations. The biological instantiation of CU-D2 (Coherence Drive Principle).

**Coherence efficiency (η_C).** The ratio C(x)/Φ(x), measuring how much coherence is maintained per unit of dissipation. Biological systems that survive maintain adequate coherence efficiency.

**Coherence functional (C(x)).** A scalar measure of integrated biological viability defined as $C(x) = A(x) \cdot I(x)$, where A(x) is adequacy and I(x) is integration. High C(x) corresponds to states supporting coordinated function, persistence, and repair; $C(x) = 0$ corresponds to loss of biological identity.

**Coherence gradient (∇C).** The gradient of the coherence functional over state space, defining directions in which coherence increases or decreases. Biological systems navigate this landscape without explicitly computing it.

**Coherence landscape.** The topography of the coherence functional over state space. Peaks correspond to highly coherent configurations (attractors); valleys correspond to fragmentation or collapse; ridges correspond to transitions between attractors.

**Constraint manifold (K_t).** The set of viable future states accessible to a system at time t. Biological identity is the continuity of K across time — identity persists when D(K_{t+1}, K_t) ≈ 0, even as the physical state x(t) changes substantially.

**Dissipation (Φ(x)).** The rate of entropy export required to maintain a system's current state. Coherence maintenance has an irreducible thermodynamic cost: the system must export entropy to its environment.

**Integration (I(x)).** A measure of mutual support among constraint satisfactions, composed of coupling (shared dependencies), synergy (mutual information), and robustness (cascade resistance). The composite measure I(x) = (γ · S · R)^(1/3) distinguishes genuinely coherent systems from aggregates of independent subsystems.

**Local—Global Coherence Principle.** The requirement that global coherence demands coherence at each scale and integration across scales. High coherence at one scale that destroys coherence at another results in low C_global (CU-FP4).

**Recurrence dominance.** The dynamical criterion for the abiogenesis threshold: P(s_{t+1} ∈ L \| s_t ∈ L) > P(s_{t+1} ∈ L \| s_t ∉ L). When this condition is met, the system's continued presence in a living-like region becomes self-reinforcing.

**Viability constraints.** The set of conditions {$V_1$, $V_2$, \ldots , $V_m$} that must be satisfied for continued biological function. Examples include metabolic constraints, structural constraints, regulatory constraints, and thermal constraints.

# About the Author

Gaura Kiśora Dās Rader was raised from birth in a Gaudiya Vaishnava spiritual community, where daily temple practice shaped his earliest development. At five, he entered a traditional gurukula — a residential school rooted in pre-dawn prayer, chanting, and the study of ancient scriptures — and remained in contemplative education through his mid-teens. Shortly after he turned 18, he dedicated himself to full-time monastic life as a teacher and practitioner, a path he followed into his late twenties.

He then pursued formal academic training — an MA in Philosophy from the University of Florida and doctoral work in Social Psychology at Ohio University — not as a departure from his contemplative formation but as an effort to build the conceptual and empirical tools it lacked. His research spans the philosophy of logic, moral philosophy, and moral psychology.

Due to circumstances in his personal life, Gaura was forced to leave the doctoral path. But the distance from academia turned out to be a blessing in disguise. Stepping away, he could finally see what he couldn't from inside the institution — the harm that the methodology and assumptions of scientific materialism were doing to the project of human inquiry and the project of human progress. Coherence Universalism grew out of that clarity: not as an academic exercise, but as an integrative response to limitations he had lived from both contemplative and scholarly sides.

Gaura is the founder and Director of Research at the Heaven≡Earth Foundation, a research and public-benefit organization based in Athens, Ohio dedicated to advancing coherence through the integration of scientific insight, spiritual understanding, and practical systems. He teaches Embodied Coherence — a movement practice integrating rope flow, qigong, yoga, and dance — in Athens, where he lives with his family. The Coherence Universalism series represents the culmination of a lifelong journey.

*For the complete Coherence Universalism series and supporting materials, visit heavenearthfoundation.org.*

www.ingramcontent.com/pod-product-compliance
Lightning Source LLC
LaVergne TN
LVHW051010080826
845145LV00009B/2556
*9781972429020*